ADVENT
CHRISTMAS
GRACE

Daily Gospel Reflections

By the Daughters of Saint Paul

BOOKS & MEDIA
Boston

Library of Congress Cataloging-in-Publication Data

Advent Christmas grace : daily gospel reflections / [compiled] by the Daughters of St. Paul.

    pages cm

  ISBN 978-0-8198-0841-7 (pbk.) -- ISBN 0-8198-0841-5 (pbk.)

  1. Bible. Gospels--Devotional literature. 2. Advent--Prayers and devotions. 3. Christmas--Prayers and devotions. 4. Epiphany--Prayers and devotions. 5. Catholic Church--Prayers and devotions. 6. Catholic Church. Lectionary for Mass (U.S.) I. Daughters of St. Paul.
  BS2555.54.A38 2015
  242'.332--dc23

                            2015017387

Cover design by Rosana Usselmann

Cover photo by Mary Emmanual Alves, FSP

Interior photos: p. 4, Jack Hazut/jhm@isrealimage.com; p. 82, Mary Emmanuel Alves, FSP

Published by Pauline Books & Media, 50 Saint Paul's Avenue, Boston, MA 02130-3491

Printed in the U.S.A.

www.pauline.org

Pauline Books & Media is the publishing house of the Daughters of St. Paul, an international congregation of women religious serving the Church with the communications media.

1 2 3 4 5 6 7 8 9   19 18 17 16 15

Contents

∴ · · · · · · · · · · · · ∴

How to Use This Book

∴ · · · · · · · · · · · ∴

Come, Lord Jesus!

Advent is the short and appealing liturgical season that helps us prepare for Christmas. Its spirit of expectation and eager waiting evokes in our hearts a desire for Christ's coming in grace. In this book, members of the Daughters of St. Paul share their reflections on the Gospel readings for the Advent and Christmas seasons, which concludes with the feast of the Baptism of the Lord. Our Founder, Blessed James Alberione, encouraged everyone to "take delight in the Gospel." In the liturgy, the Church presents passages from the Gospel for us to ponder and pray over, encouraging us to look into our hearts and the heart of the God who comes.

These pages are based on *Lectio Divina* (holy reading), which is a way of praying with Scripture. Many methods of doing this have developed since the time of early monasticism. Here, the sisters use a simple framework that allows the Word of God to make room in our minds and hearts

The first step, *Lectio* (reading), is to read the day's Gospel passage from a missal or Bible. Read it a few times slowly, perhaps especially noticing the phrase or verse that is listed under the *Meditatio* section.

Next, the *Meditatio* (meditation) expands the meaning of a phrase from the passage and explores what it is saying to us today—what God asks of us, or challenges us with, or offers to us. After reading the meditation, take as much time as you wish to reflect on it.

The *Oratio* (prayer) can help you talk to God about what has arisen in your heart, so that the time of prayer becomes a conversation, not just a time to think. God has spoken in the Scripture. We hear the invitation in our meditation, but now a response is called for. Our response is not just to say, "Yes, I want to do as you are asking me," but also to say, "Help me do it, Lord!"

The short line under *Contemplatio* (contemplation) is a way of extending this time of prayer into life. You can silently repeat the line throughout the day to help deepen the intimacy with the Lord that you experienced in prayer.

May your Advent and Christmas be grace-filled and abundantly blessed!

Liturgical Calendar

⁘ · · · · · · · · · · · ⁘

Note to the reader: Advent begins four Sundays before December 25. The first Sunday of Advent begins the Church's liturgical year. The readings are assigned for the weekdays of Advent by week and day (e.g., Tuesday of the Second Week). A special series of readings begins on December 17. The Sunday readings follow a three-year cycle (A, B, or C) as indicated in the chart below. Before Epiphany, the weekday readings are assigned by date, beginning on January 2. In the United States and Canada, Epiphany is celebrated on the Sunday between January 2 and January 8. After Epiphany, the readings are assigned by day of the week (eg. Monday after Epiphany). However in places where Epiphany is still celebrated on January 6, the readings for the days after it are given by date (eg. January 7 through 12).

YEAR	CYCLE
2016	Cycle C
2017	Cycle A
2018	Cycle B
2019	Cycle C
2020	Cycle A
2021	Cycle B
2022	Cycle C
2023	Cycle A

During Advent,
we long for the coming
of the awaited Messiah—
in Bethlehem,
at the end of time,
and in each human heart ...

Sunday of the First Week of Advent — A

⁙ ⋯⋯⋯⋯ ⁙

Lectio

Matthew 24:37–44

Meditatio

". . . your Lord . . ."

This startling reading from Matthew certainly gets our attention. It alerts us that this first day of Advent ushers us into an entirely new season. The liturgy warns: Pay attention! Stay awake! When they least expect it, chaotic events upset people's lives, with dire consequences: "one will be taken, and one will be left." But what can it mean? Jesus exhorts us again and again: Stay awake! Be prepared! You do not know the hour! The warnings may alarm us, but they are meant to prepare us for the coming of Christ.

References to Noah and the flood unsettle me. Had I been there, would I have believed Noah? If I had been among the women grinding at the mill, would I have been taken or left? Then Jesus speaks of a burglar, noting that the owner of a house would prevent a robbery if he knew when it would happen. What do all these references have to do with me? Chapter 24 is about the end of the world and the second coming of Jesus. Jesus is coming again! That is why we must stay awake.

This Gospel reminds me of the wise and foolish virgins with their oil lamps. They all fall asleep. That somehow makes me feel better. When I am really sleepy I can hardly keep my eyes open! But some virgins are better prepared than the others. Although all the virgins fall asleep, the wise virgins had anticipated a long wait and had brought extra oil. And they are ready with their lighted lamps to welcome the bridegroom when he finally arrives.

Today's text includes a subtle word that makes this reading much more personal and offers us hope: "For you do not know on which day your Lord will come." *Your* Lord. You are my Lord, Jesus, our Lord. You are no stranger, no uncaring, unfamiliar master. You are my Lord and my God. I too want to be present, Jesus, waiting for you: awake and ready anytime you want to approach me.

Oratio

Jesus, it is no thief or burglar who is breaking in; it is you. You study the fortress I've built around myself, scanning my ramparts for that one fatal flaw. Be that thief in the night and come! Burgle me, Lord! Break through the walls. You are my Lord and my Savior and desire only my good. I want nothing between us, nothing to separate us, especially the defenses I have built up over the years. Jesus, break through them and allow me to really know you.

Contemplatio

Jesus, you are my Lord and my Savior.

Sunday of the First Week of Advent — B

∴ · · · · · · · · · · · ∴

Lectio

Mark 13:33–37

Meditatio

"Watch!"

Today Advent begins with the repeated cry: "Watch!" This word appears four times in today's Gospel. Jesus doesn't simply say, "Wait for me to come." Rather, he wants us to actively anticipate his return, to prepare everything to celebrate his arrival!

Perhaps we find ourselves torn between two responses to this command of the Lord. Perhaps lately we have been indifferent toward spiritual realities, worn down by the endless activities and worries that fill our hearts and haunt our thoughts. Jesus' "Watch!" gently nudges us from our tired sleep and rekindles our enthusiasm in our walk with the Lord. On the other hand, with fewer than thirty "shopping days 'til Christmas," we may dread the endless check-out lines, traffic snarls, unpredictable weather, and preparations for Christmas parties and gifts. Jesus' invitation to "Watch!" reassures us: he asks only for a childlike excitement about his love for us that gives our lives meaning.

Advent is a time to check our spiritual eyesight. To what degree are we watching and waiting? Do we have 20/20 vision? How excited are we?

To prepare for Christmas you may make lists, schedules, menus, and plans. Today, take a moment to write down some concrete spiritual plans as you watch for the coming of the Lord. Advent is a time for envisioning change. What is your image of a deeply Christ-filled life? Choose two concrete changes in your life that would make you excited and give more meaning to your following of the Lord. Get your vision down to a concrete plan by answering the five basic questions: Who? What? Where? When? Why?

Each Advent morning, watch for the Lord by rereading your plan, preparing for the day ahead. Watch for just one day at a time; Jesus will come not only upon his return at the end of time, but he will also come today ... not just once, but many times. If you watch you will be surprised at how often he is here!

Oratio

Jesus, Advent is such a lovely time. I'm getting excited that this year it could be different for me. Help me keep the excitement of a child in the midst of the hustle and bustle. Give me the eyes to see you every time you walk into my life. Amen.

Contemplatio

Jesus, I am watching!

Sunday of the First Week of Advent — C

∴ · · · · · · · · · · · ∴

Lectio

Luke 21:25–28, 34–36

Meditatio

> *"But when these signs begin to happen,*
> *stand erect and raise your heads because your redemption is at hand."*

A few radio stations began playing Christmas music weeks ago. The malls and department stores are decked out for the holiday gift season. Lights twinkle in the trees around town. And here we are starting Advent with one of the classic "hellfire and brimstone" texts. Christians! Sometimes we're a contrary bunch.

Contrary indeed. In the midst of dire warnings about signs in the sun, moon, and stars, and an exhortation to avoid carousing and drunkenness, Jesus interjects a new, unexpected note: "... stand erect and raise your heads because your redemption is at hand."

The end of the world as we know it is coming—but if Jesus is to be believed, it is not a doom and gloom event. He reminds us that we are looking forward to a time of redemption and salvation in its full expression. This gives us the confidence to stand and look to the future with joyful expectation.

Today we begin Advent, the liturgical time of waiting. In a certain sense, we always live in advent expectation. Christ has come, and yet we also claim that Christ will come again. The kingdom of God is in our midst, and yet we pray each day: "Thy Kingdom come." Theologians speak of the time of "already and the not yet."

Our redemption is at hand. It is already here. Jesus was born in Bethlehem. He died on Calvary, and, most significantly, he rose again at Easter. In this sense, the redemption is an accomplished fact. Viewed from another perspective, however, the redemption is being worked out in our daily thoughts, choices, words, and actions. In this sense, too, our redemption is at hand. It is lived out in the here-and-now moments of life.

Christmas is coming. The signs are everywhere. Christ is coming. Are the signs evident in our lives?

Oratio

Lord, sometimes I am annoyed and at other times I am amused at the contrast between the prayerful unfolding of Advent's great themes and the gauntlet of December rituals expected in society. Help me to keep my focus on the signs of your coming. You come in gentle, hidden ways. Don't let me miss you when you come in the disguise of people I may be tempted to ignore: the poor, the weak, the suffering, the person who annoys or insults me...

Contemplatio

Christ has come. Christ will come again.

Monday of the First Week of Advent

∴ ⋯⋯⋯⋯ ∵

Lectio

Matthew 8:5–11

Meditatio

"I will come . . ."

In the movie *August Rush*, the eleven-year-old orphan Evan Taylor hopes to be reunited with his birth parents, whom he has never known. His parents, Lyla and Louis, fall in love but are separated. Lyla has a child, but her father gives the child up for adoption without Lyla's knowledge. With the vision possible only to the human heart, Evan clings to the hope he will one day be reunited with his parents. Evan can be for us an icon of Advent hope. He longs to know he is not alone, to know that he is loved.

During Advent, we also long for the coming of the awaited Messiah—in Bethlehem, at the end of time, and in each human heart, including our own. Like Evan, we also cry out: "Come!"

Similarly, the centurion in today's Gospel pleads with Jesus to heal a sick servant. The centurion trusts Jesus so much that he believes Jesus' word has power to bring relief and healing. Situations of pain or paralysis in our own lives can open us up to cry out for healing. This desire prompts us to reach out to those we trust: a spouse, a close friend or relative, a parent, mentor, spiritual guide, God. Sometimes a simple word or gesture from someone significant reassures us that we are not alone. How powerful are the words: "I'll be right there," or, "I am with you."

Ponder for a moment the first three words of Jesus' response to the centurion's request: "I will come ..." Every time we call out to him, our loving God says the same thing: "I will come." Jesus manifests his desire to come and be with us not just at certain moments, but all the time. Just as Evan Taylor's hopeful expectation for reunion is finally fulfilled, our longing for God's presence will also be fulfilled. The Lord reassures us: "I am with you always ..." (Mt 28:20).

Oratio

Lord, come anew into this heart made by you, hungry for you. Come into my heart, my mind, my life, my entire being, body and soul. Heal what is broken in me; give life to what is paralyzed within me. I believe you can do all things, and that you want to come and heal. Like the centurion, who asked for healing for his servant, I also ask you to bless and heal those for whom I pray today, especially for: *(pause to mention names)*.

Come, Emmanuel, God with us.

Contemplatio

"Come, O Lord. Do not delay."

Tuesday of the First Week of Advent

⁚ · · · · · · · · · · · ·⁚

Lectio

Luke 10:21–24

Meditatio

"At that very moment he rejoiced. . . ."

In the verses that precede this Scripture passage the seventy-two disciples have just returned from their mission. They are rejoicing for all they did in Jesus' name. At this Jesus tells them they should rejoice because "their names are written in heaven." Immediately following this we read, "At that very moment he rejoiced [in] the holy Spirit...."

Jesus lives in such continuous intimacy with the Father and the Holy Spirit that he does not hesitate to praise God. This is not one of those moments when Jesus goes off to pray by himself. Instead, in the midst of Jesus' realization of the Father's work, the Holy Spirit stirs in him and he praises the Father aloud.

The author of the Gospel relates that Jesus praises God with the seventy-two gathered around him. The immediacy of his prayer tells us that Jesus is not ashamed to show his intimate relationship with God to those who are gathered there. How would we ever know the level of intimacy in the

Trinity if Jesus had not allowed us to see this moment of prayer? In his own profoundly simple manner, Jesus allows us to glimpse what joy and happiness are. They are by-products of a life lived in communion with God.

This moment of intense and spontaneous prayer also reveals to us that we must share the faith we have received. Just as Jesus shares this intimate moment with his disciples and us, we are called to share our faith with our brothers and sisters.

Being Christ-like doesn't mean showing off for others by enumerating the times I pray or do some corporal or spiritual work of mercy—but it does mean living publicly a faith-filled witness. Am I living as Jesus did? Am I living a life of faith in public action or do I keep my faith private and to myself?

Oratio

Father, Son, and Holy Spirit, I wish to live in deeper communion with you during this Advent season. I humbly ask for the grace to place my relationship with you at my center so that you may touch and permeate all I say and do. In seeing me, may people truly see you at work in me and give you praise. May I not hesitate to recognize your work in me and in my brothers and sisters, and may I give you praise for it.

Contemplatio

Permeate me and mold me, Father, Son, and Holy Spirit.

Wednesday of the First Week of Advent

∴ ·············· ∵

Lectio

Matthew 15:29–37

Meditatio

> *"My heart is moved with pity for the crowd."*

Today's Gospel visibly demonstrates Jesus' compassion in word and action. After days of following the Master, the crowd longs for his presence, his words, and his saving deeds. Jesus also knows the people are hungry! "My heart is moved with pity…."

As the Teacher climbs the mountain and sits before the crowd, the suffering of the sick and the needs of the people stirred his heart with pity. His saving touch heals the physically challenged and those who suffered many kinds of sickness. With seven loaves and a few fish, Jesus multiplies the food so the people will not "collapse on the way."

The healing of the sick and the feeding of the four thousand show clearly how profoundly God embraces our human condition in Jesus Christ. The heart of God understands the physical suffering, pain, and weakness we experience! He is not only a God who is "for" us in our need, but who experienced hunger and physical pain in his own flesh.

Perhaps images of Lourdes fill our imagination when we read this Gospel. Men, women, and children who suffer from every kind of physical, emotional, and mental illness seek spiritual and physical healing at Lourdes. Accompanied by caregivers and family members, the sick assemble as the Eucharist is celebrated, received, and adored. Jesus' heart again "is moved with pity" for them as it was on that mountain in Galilee. Lourdes is a place of hope because the presence of God is so deeply felt in prayer, word, and sacrament. How completely Jesus embraces human weakness is so visible and deeply moving at Lourdes.

Jesus never runs away from our pain, sin, or human messiness, but he embraces them in tenderness and mercy. We can bring to our Savior's compassionate heart whatever weighs us down, wherever we live!

Oratio

Jesus, companion and friend, walk with me when I feel I cannot go on. Feed me with your word and the Eucharist so the needs and hungers of my heart will be fed. Bring healing to whatever is sick in me. May my words and actions give hope to those who journey with me and who feel overwhelmed by problems and concerns. Satisfy the hunger of the world's poor with bread, and the hunger of all people for love and a meaningful life. May the Eucharist be the icon through which I see the needs and hungers of others.

Contemplatio

Jesus, you satisfy the hungers of my heart.

Thursday of the First Week of Advent

:· ············ ·:

Lectio

Matthew 7:21, 24–27

Meditatio

> *"Everyone who listens to these words of mine and acts on them will be like a wise man who built his house on rock."*

In today's Gospel, Jesus gives us an important life lesson: nothing happens unless we act. It isn't enough merely to listen to Jesus. Listening is important, but it's only the first step. As Scripture says, God's word is living and active. It prods us into action. It is easier to talk about something than it is to roll up our sleeves and get to work. As long as seeds stay in their packet, they'll never grow. But plant and water them, and soon a beautiful garden will grow. Our lives will bear fruit to the extent that we turn our words into deeds.

In baptism, we became members of Christ and were filled with the Holy Spirit. We have two choices about what we can do with that divine life given so abundantly. One choice is to let it lie dormant. If we choose that path, we'll remain perpetual infants in the spiritual life. We'll be like those seeds that just stay in the packet and never grow into anything. At the end of our life, we'll *say,* "Lord, Lord." But God will ask us what we *did* with the gift he gave us.

There is another choice: to listen to Jesus and then to act on his words. You don't have to do big things, showy things, things that attract attention. Instead, practice love of God and love of neighbor. Pray every day. Follow the commandments. Do some small act of kindness. Participate in the Sunday Eucharist each week. If you wish to turn your life around spiritually, start with something small. Take some desire that you've had about growing spiritually and make it a goal. For example, have you always wanted to read the Bible but been daunted at its sheer size? Of the twenty-seven books in the New Testament, seventeen of them have six chapters or fewer. Try reading those first. Once you get started, you won't want to stop.

Oratio

Lord Jesus, help me to listen to the words you speak to me and to act on them. I want to put my life in your hands, and I trust in your plan for me. In the Gospel, you tell me that if I listen to your words and put them into practice, I will be like those wise persons who build their lives on rock. When the winds of life threaten to blow me down, I will not fear because you are my rock.

Contemplatio

"Not everyone who says to me, 'Lord, Lord,' will enter the kingdom of heaven, but only the one who does the will of my Father in heaven."

Friday of the First Week of Advent

∴ ⋯⋯⋯⋯ ∴

Lectio

Matthew 9:27–31

Meditatio

> *"[A]s Jesus passed on from there,*
> *two blind men followed...."*

To enter into the heart of this Gospel passage, you might remember a classic game: stand at the entrance of your living room, blindfolded, and then try to make your way to the other end of the room. Now try doing this with a partner. It probably won't be easier. You'll be laughing so much that you won't be able to recall exactly where the coffee table is.

Today's Gospel passage recounts a similar scene. Two blind men find out Jesus is passing by and they both begin to follow him, crying out together for healing. The two blind men take a huge risk. Imagine how foolish they must have looked as they made their way through the crowd, bumping into people as they went.

This is not a case of the "blind leading the blind." Instead, the two men give each other light, guidance, and courage as they both seek to meet Jesus. They lead each other by the light of desire.

Let's take a moment to shift our gaze from the blind men to Jesus. How does he react when he sees and hears these two men stumbling toward him? Perhaps their faith and determination surprised him. As Jesus sees them awkwardly making their way toward him, he must feel compassion and love for them.

When God sees our desire for him and his goodness, when he sees how we rush toward him, perhaps stumbling on the way, he cannot hold himself back. God says, "Let it be done for you," just as Jesus says to the blind men who seek him out.

Jesus is inviting us to risk allowing our deepest desires and perhaps our deepest darkness to draw us closer to him. He stands knocking on the door of our heart. Will we let him in?

Oratio

Jesus, I am amazed to discover that the areas of my life that have been the most difficult are now leading me closer to you. Although I feel shame in my weakness, it is precisely my weakness that draws me closer to you. It is my weakness that helps me take the risk of running to you. I truly desire to come before you now and to show you my blindness, so as to receive your light. I desire you, Jesus.

Contemplatio

"Let it be done for you."

Saturday of the First Week of Advent

⁘ ············ ⁖

Lectio

Matthew 9:35—10:1, 5a, 6–8

Meditatio

> *"… his heart was moved with pity for them*
> *because they were troubled and abandoned.…"*

Jesus comes and lives among us, as one of us. With his own eyes he sees human misery, all forms of pain and desolation. He dares to face the reality of human suffering. He conquers evil by doing good; he restores life and brings hope.

When Jesus looks at the crowds who follow him, he sees the people as God sees them—betrayed and abandoned, like sheep without a shepherd, as Jeremiah describes the Chosen People: "Lost sheep were my people, their shepherds misled them … losing their way to the fold" (Jer 50:6). In the Old Testament, God is called the "Shepherd of Israel" (Ps 80:1), who "feeds his flock" (Is 40:11). And God says: "I myself will look after and tend my sheep … rescue them … I myself will pasture my sheep.… The lost I will seek out, the strayed I will bring back, the injured I will bind up, the sick I will heal, shepherding them rightly" (Ez 34:11–16).

Jesus not only feels compassion for them, but he also knows they need a shepherd to love and guide them. He calls himself the "Good Shepherd" (Jn 10:11). As a true shepherd, he dwells continually in the midst of God's People. He seeks the strays and wants to lead them all. He sees that the time is ripe to gather the flock into God's kingdom. However, the workers are few. Jesus invites his disciples to pray to God, the Lord of the harvest, for more laborers. He then calls twelve men and invites them to share his same mission—to proclaim the arrival of God's kingdom and to heal every ill. Jesus fulfills God's promise: "I will appoint over you shepherds after my own heart, who will shepherd you wisely and prudently" (Jer 3:15). Later, Peter exhorts those entrusted with a pastoral office: "Tend the flock of God in your midst … as God would have it, not for shameful profit but eagerly" (I Pt 5:2).

Oratio

Jesus, you see that the harvest for your kingdom is ripe. Give all your disciples the courage to face the reality of human suffering, to see the needs of others as you do. Replace our minds with yours. Give us the compassion and desire to meet our real needs in love. Replace our hearts with yours. Give us the strength to do good to others so that we may all come to you and enter your kingdom. Replace our wills with yours.

Contemplatio

Jesus, allow me to see and meet the true needs of others with loving compassion

December 8 — Immaculate Conception

:⋅ ⋯⋯⋯⋯ ⋅:

Lectio

Luke 1:26–38

Meditatio

> *"Mary pondered what sort of greeting this might be."*

What do we know about Mary prior to this wonderful encounter with God's messenger? Nothing. We do not even know if she had been praying. We are simply introduced to her as a betrothed virgin living in Nazareth of Galilee. The text gives no age, no description, no parentage, but just a name—a common name at that.

The Gospel introduces her visitor as the angel Gabriel, sent by God. Interestingly, the text says that *upon arriving* the angel spoke to her. It sounds as if he came into town and approached her house as any human visitor would. This begs for more information about the angel Gabriel, but we are given no more. The heart of this Gospel story lies in their dialogue. Everything else is incidental. The angel addresses Mary as *"Hail, full of grace! The Lord is with you."* The greeting troubles Mary greatly. It sets her off balance and she begins to ponder it deeply. Seeing her expression the angel continues, *"Do not be afraid, Mary, for you have found favor with God."* Then he outlines God's plan: she will conceive a son and name him

Jesus. He will do great things and be called God's Son; he will inherit David's throne and reign forever. Mary does not object to this fantastic message, but she poses a very practical question. How this will happen, she asks, *"since I have no relations with a man."* Gabriel assures her that this will be the work of the Holy Spirit who will come to her. Because of this, the child will be holy, the Son of God. As reassurance he tells her that Elizabeth, her barren cousin, is six months pregnant. At this Mary offers a stunningly simple reply, *"Behold, I am the handmaid of the Lord. May it be done to me according to your word."* With that the angel's mission is accomplished and he leaves her. Mary has taken the messenger at his word. Her yes is worthier because she said it knowing some details but going mostly on faith. We will never be asked for a similar agreement by God, but we should ponder how we respond to his requests and invitations as we hear them in our hearts.

Oratio

Lord, keep our hearts always young before you, as was Mary's heart, attentive and generous. Let us, too, find favor with you. Sometimes your visitations are troubling and your messages difficult to hear. Sometimes you are asking us to bear suffering, sickness, even death; sometimes it is misunderstanding, great trials, or heartaches. May our response to you always mirror that of our mother, Mary. *You see that I am your servant. Do with me as you will.* Amen.

Contemplatio

May it be done to me according to your will.

Sunday of the Second Week of Advent — A

⁘ ············ ⁘

Lectio

Matthew 3:1–12

Meditatio

> *"God can raise up children to Abraham from these stones."*

These words of John the Baptist seem to spring from frustration rather than from anger. He is chiding these learned and observant men, the scribes and Pharisees, for their lack of comprehension. They are both the children and the leaders of Israel. Steeped in the law, these men know the prophecies, rely on the promises, hope for redemption. At this very moment the promised redemption is about to dawn. Although they are face to face with it, they do not recognize the gift of God's visitation.

Advent is meant to be our John the Baptist. We let him remind us that we are people to whom God has given so many gifts. But do we find ourselves a bit complacent, relying on the fact that we are baptized, confirmed, married, consecrated, or anointed? Do we "presume" that all is well because we are Christian? The Lord wants us to be fully alive, to practice a vibrant faith, and to keep our hearts pure. The season of Advent invites us to examine our lives. It is our time to listen to John's words and to act upon them, to ready ourselves for "the One who is coming," the One who brings a "baptism of the Holy Spirit and fire."

Scripture often uses the image of stones to make a point. Stones represent our vocation as parts of God's building: "[Y]ou are ... built upon the foundation of the apostles and prophets, with Christ Jesus himself as the capstone" (Eph 2:19–20; see also 1 Cor 3:10ff.). Peter was called the rock upon which the Church would be built (see Mt 16:18), and we ourselves are the very stones. Abraham's faith remains firm in the edifice of Christ's holy People, the Church. It is for us to be firm and strong in our faith, to be stones that cry out in gratitude and praise (see Lk 19:40).

Oratio

Lord, you are my rock and my Redeemer. Teach me to rely on your strength in my weakness, in your firmness when I falter. Do not let me be complacent and inattentive. Rather, in this holy season when we celebrate your coming among us as man, let me be attentive and engaged, aware of your gifts, and intent on doing my best toward building up your kingdom Amen.

Contemplatio

"A voice of one crying out in the desert, 'Prepare the way of the Lord, make straight his paths.'"

Sunday of the Second Week of Advent — B

∴ · · · · · · · · · · · ∴

Lectio

Mark 1:1–8

Meditatio

> *"The beginning of the Gospel ..."*

Beginnings are generally small, even insignificant. Nightfall begins when the first faint star appears. A world-changing technology may begin in a flash of insight entirely hidden to all but the thinker. A life-changing love may have its origin in a subtle glance whose potential could never be fathomed by the two who exchange it. Advent celebrates just this kind of beginning, one bursting with possibilities.

The Gospel itself, "the power of God for salvation" (see Rom 1:16), begins with a solitary voice in the desert. Those who heard that call probably thought the eccentric John, with his camel hair and locusts, was the focal point of what was about to begin. But John is not staging an event as if he were launching a new product line or planning an inauguration. Instead, he claims to be no more than an advance messenger; the "one mightier" is drawing near. This is why John pares his existence down to the essentials. This is why John insists on a symbolic baptism of repentance and a confession that is both an admission of sin and a proclamation of hope and praise: John is preparing the way of the Lord. This is the Lord who had spoken through the prophets, anticipating the utter newness that was "impossible to human beings, but not for God" (see Mk 10:27): "I will give you a new heart and place a new spirit within you" (Ez 36:26).

For Mark, it isn't only a written account that starts, as all books do, from "the beginning": it is the Gospel itself that is just beginning, even now. We even find a new beginning at the end of Mark's Gospel, where the Lord sends us, like the apostles, to proclaim the Gospel to every creature (see Mk 16:15). Mark is telling us that the entire written Gospel is the first breath of something startlingly new.

Oratio

Lord, I admit to a certain amount of fear in the face of what is new, even when I secretly know that the old and familiar no longer work. During this Advent week, let me hear your word in a new way. Renew me in mind and heart so that I will be able to respond to you in peace. Then I will give you praise for the great things you are bringing about before my very eyes!

Contemplatio

Lord, even here, even now, you are doing something new!

Sunday of the Second Week of Advent — C

:• ·········· •:

Lectio

Luke 3:1–6

Meditatio

> *"[T]he word of God came to John ... in the desert."*

It's not surprising that God's word came to John in the desert. Scripture tells us that Israel's early history abounded with desert experiences.

Abraham receives God's promise of descendants out in the open, beneath a sky strewn with stars. Sleeping in a barren landscape, with a stone for his pillow, Jacob experiences the Lord's glory and reassuring presence as he set out on his journey to Haran. Moses first encounters God when a voice calls to him from a bush blazing on Mount Sinai. In that same desert God later molds the Israelites into a people.

Desert experiences are also part of the Church's heritage. The seasons of Advent and Lent remind us of this.

I hope that during this Advent each of us will have an opportunity to create within ourselves our own "desert," where we can meet the Lord and walk with him. In that desert we can share our concerns and his, ask for light and guidance, savor Jesus' presence, and deepen our awareness that he is the "reason for the season."

But what about the frenetic pre-Christmas bustle? God can reach us through that, too. He may speak through a child, a spouse, a friend, a colleague, a sales clerk…. He may communicate through circumstances that impel us to reassess our values and priorities, or through the silent cries of the needy poor and neglected elderly.

Advent is one of the "strong times" in the Church year when God's presence may be more intensely felt and his will more clearly understood. I want to be alert—always ready to respond.

What am I being called to do this Advent? To perform special acts of kindness? To sacrifice my own preferences for the sake of others? Or something else?

Oratio

O Emmanuel, the expected of the nations and their Savior, draw me close to you during this Advent. Help me to experience your gentle presence. Enable me to follow your inspirations and to share your love and peace with others. Through me, may my family, friends, and acquaintances grow to appreciate more deeply the true meaning of this holy season. May we all see beyond blinking holiday lights to the radiance of the star.

Contemplatio

"And all flesh shall see the salvation of God."

Monday of the Second Week of Advent

⁚ ············ ⁚

Lectio

Luke 5:17–26

Meditatio

> *"When he saw their faith, he said,*
> *'As for you, your sins are forgiven.'"*

As I read this Gospel, I am struck by the simple love and determination of these unnamed men for their paralyzed friend. They are not idly interested in the possibility of witnessing a miracle. They are men with a purpose, whose love will take them to great lengths to see their friend well again. They are also men who have great faith in the power of God at work through Jesus.

In one translation, the word for "faith" in this Gospel is translated as "trust." I like this way of thinking about faith. We hear the word "faith" so often that at times it might bounce off our minds and hearts without hitting the mark. We assume we have faith—after all, we go to Mass on Sundays and say our prayers, right? But in a world where true relationships can be hard to find, the word "trust" can hit our ears and minds in a different way. We know the risks and rewards contained in that simple word.

Perhaps what strikes me most in this Gospel is Jesus' response to the great trust these men have in him. Seeing their perseverance and hope as a sign of great faith, he is moved to action, healing the paralyzed man in spirit and in body.

What might this mean for us? Perhaps it means that we, too, have this gift and this responsibility to bring one another before the Lord in faith. At times, each of us walks through the dark valley, feeling that God is far away and prayer is next to impossible. In these moments of spiritual and emotional paralysis, what would it be like to remember and to believe that my family and friends can bring me before Jesus in faith when I can no longer bring myself?

It remains a message of great hope to realize that I, too, can do this for those whom I love.

Oratio

Lord Jesus, this Advent you are calling me to a deeper trust in you—to a trust that believes in the power of prayer. It can be so painful to watch loved ones wander farther and farther away from you, or fall deeper and deeper into emotional darkness and pain. Today, I am bringing before you those in my life who seem to be wandering in darkness. You are the light that dawns in all hearts. Thank you for your healing light and for the power of your Spirit at work in our lives.

Contemplatio

Jesus, I trust in you.

Tuesday of the Second Week of Advent

∴ · · · · · · · · · · · ∴

Lectio

Matthew 18:12–14

Meditatio

"What is your opinion?"

What is my opinion? Would I risk the safety of ninety-nine sheep to go looking for one? Would I spend precious time and resources doing that?

In the context of Matthew 18, it is clear that this passage refers to the Christian community. Jesus makes a distinction between those who stray and those who cause harm to others or who give scandal (see Mt 18:5–10).

Those who stray are often the marginalized—perhaps those on the fringes, the drug addict or alcoholic, the immigrant—whoever for some reason is not able to be in complete communion with the community of believers. Jesus would seek these people out to try to bring them back.

He would spend precious time and resources trying to rehabilitate them. He would risk the safety of those who have not strayed. The question he asks, though, is: Would we? Would I? What is my opinion?

There are many reasons why a person may choose to no longer follow Jesus in the community of believers. The first reaction of others may sometimes be judgment and harsh criticism of the one straying. Some, particularly family members, suffer because of the separation. But the vulnerability that one experiences because of being isolated makes it possible for that person to accept divine love in a way that was not previously possible. If we look at it this way, we may be more inclined to be hopeful for the person, rather than judgmental or sad. It may be someone else right now; it may be me tomorrow.

If it is imperative for the shepherd to search out and to try to persuade the person to return, it is just as imperative for that person to find a welcoming community on his or her return. I wonder whether the prospect of such a welcome would hasten the stray's return. Thus, both shepherd and community have equally essential roles to play in this search and rescue process.

Oratio

Jesus, help me to recognize those who have strayed and those parts of me which may not allow me to follow you within the community of believers. Change judgment to mercy and hope. Make my heart like your heart so others may be touched by you through me. And instead of dwelling on the condition of those outside the community, may I always wait for the day of rejoicing.

Contemplatio

"For my thoughts are not your thoughts, nor are your ways my ways, says the Lord" (Is 55:8).

Wednesday of the Second Week of Advent

⁘ ············ ⁘

Lectio

Matthew 11:28–30

Meditatio

> *"Come to me, all you who labor and are burdened,*
> *and I will give you rest."*

Who cannot relate to this passage? The feeling of being tired and burdened can last all year and is simply more intense these weeks before Christmas. Yet Advent is the one time we really long to slow down and appreciate the season. We know that we celebrate at Christmas the mystery that holds for us great joy: the birth of our Savior. Children are innately happy, filled with eager anticipation—even the secular world celebrates this season of joy. We long to savor the gift, to get away from the frenetic pace so often connected with this season.

My parents, ever my spiritual models, years ago made the simple decision that they would no longer go the expensive and exasperating mall-crawling, gift-giving route. They give a donation to charity, commit to daily Mass, and spend the rest of Advent a little more calm and less burdened as they visit family and friends.

In the midst of this hectic season, Jesus invites us to take his "light" and "easy" yoke upon our shoulders. But to take up his yoke, we shall have to lay down our own—there is no room for two. We shall have to lay down those "unnecessary anxieties" that weigh on us and squelch our joy. Jesus invites us to let go of whatever weighs us down. In my case this means my perfectionism, worry, unrealistic expectations. The meal doesn't have to be the best ever; sending cards can be a time of prayer for each person I write to; decorating can be done simply. If I could let go of useless anxieties, I could give more attention to the people and projects that genuinely merit it. I could give more time to prayer.

Only trust in the Lord will allow me to exchange my yoke for his. To accept in faith that Jesus has the compassion, wisdom, and strength to handle my burdens will allow me to let go and be free.

Oratio

Lord Jesus, I fear that if mine is the first move I will never make it. If I must divest myself of my self-made yoke before I take on yours, where will I find the strength? But if you would help me here, if you would give me the grace to trust in your love, to trust in your strength and power to provide— if you make the first move, then I will have courage. Let me taste the sweetness of your yoke so my own pales in comparison and I willingly let it go to embrace yours.

Contemplatio

Lord, help me believe your words: your yoke is easy and your burden light.

Thursday of the Second Week of Advent

∴ ⋯⋯⋯⋯ ∴

Lectio

Matthew 11:11–15

Meditatio

> *"… yet the least in the kingdom of heaven is greater than he."*

Advent is my favorite part of the liturgical year. I love the candlelight of the Advent wreath amid the darkening winter days and the sparkling Christmas lights that glow on homes and along busy streets. They remind me of the Father's promise of redemption. God is doing something new among us. The darkness of sin and sadness will soon give way to the Light of the World.

Amid all these signs of expectation—amid the Christmas trees and snowflakes and crèche scenes—the Baptist emerges as a startling figure. As I prepare for Christmas by baking cookies and sending cards to loved ones, John the Baptist appears eating locusts and wearing camel hair, preaching a stern message of repentance for sins. Today, Jesus holds him up for us as a truly great man. John had great courage and conviction. He followed the call of God to the desert, to the palaces of kings, and finally to his death. You would have to be "great" indeed to live the life of fearless integrity and fiery passion for God that John lived.

And yet, Jesus says, even I, one of the least of the kingdom of heaven, am greater than the great Baptist. What could Jesus possibly mean? How could I—with all my sparkling Christmas lights and cookie-loving ways—possibly be greater than John the Baptist?

The secret to this greatness lies not in myself, but in my relationship with Christ. God has truly done something new. Since the coming of Christ among us—the coming that John the Baptist so zealously prepared us for—we are able to share in the life of Christ. Through our baptism, we receive this new life and are welcomed into the kingdom of God. This is the precious gift of Christmas, the reason for our preparation and expectation. This sharing in the life of God is the true source of greatness.

Oratio

Jesus, as I live these days of Advent and prepare my heart for your coming, deepen my understanding of the gift of my baptism. Help me to understand what it means to share in your life. May your love reach others through my loving actions.

Contemplatio

"… you received a spirit of adoption, through which we cry, '*Abba,* Father!' The Spirit itself bears witness with our spirit that we are children of God…."

Friday of the Second Week of Advent

∴ ⋯⋯⋯⋯ ∴

Lectio

Matthew 11:16–19

Meditatio

> *"The Son of Man came eating and drinking and they said ..."*

When my siblings and I were little we would sometimes get in a contrary mood that my mom called "try-an'-please-me." No matter what my mother suggested or offered us—things to play with, snacks, or drinks—we were never satisfied.

Usually Jesus speaks of children as models of what Christians should be like (because of their simplicity and trust), but this passage evokes the idea of the contrariness of children. The crowd listening to Jesus had not been fully converted by the preaching of John—they said he must have been crazy or possessed to have adopted such an extreme lifestyle in the desert, "neither eating nor drinking." But Jesus didn't live that kind of hermit- or prophet-like existence. He lived among the people, and he ate and drank with them when they invited him to their homes. So they now accuse him of lack of moderation. "Look, he is a glutton and a drunkard ..."

He just can't win.

No matter what God does for us, no matter how many calls, opportunities, or invitations we are offered, we can always find something to complain about. We can always rationalize our way out of having to repent and change our ways.

If the pastor is good and holy, then he's too strict and doesn't understand life in the real world. If the pastor has notable human failings, then he's a hypocrite for expecting us to live a holy life. The same things can be applied to supervisors in the work place, superiors in religious communities, and so forth. It seems we always want to wiggle out from under the finger we feel is pointed at us, and the easiest way of doing that is to point at someone or something else. But Jesus invites us to a deeper wisdom by being honest with ourselves and with him.

Oratio

Jesus, this Scripture passage makes me take an honest look at myself. I can see that I do sometimes distract attention from my own limitations and failings by drawing attention to those of others. Even if I don't say anything out loud, I make excuses to myself to explain why I am not closer to being the person you have called me to be. Thankfully, you are patient with me and you never give up calling, inviting, offering possibilities for growth.

Contemplatio

Today I will respond—no excuses.

Saturday of the Second Week of Advent

∴ ⋯⋯⋯⋯ ∴

Lectio

Matthew 17:9a, 10–13

Meditatio

"Elijah will indeed come and restore all things; but I tell you that Elijah has already come, and they did not recognize him...."

Today's Gospel and first reading focus on the prophet Elijah. The disciples ask Jesus, "Why do the scribes say that Elijah must come first?" They are probably referring to the text from the prophet Malachi, "Lo, I will send you Elijah, the prophet, Before the day of the LORD comes, the great and terrible day, / To turn the hearts of the fathers to their children, and the hearts of the children to their fathers ..." (Mal 3:23–24). In answering their question, Jesus indicates that John the Baptist is the new Elijah: "I tell you that Elijah has already come, and they did not recognize him...."

When the angel Gabriel announces to Zechariah the birth of John the Baptist, the angel speaks of John as a new Elijah: "He will go before him in the spirit and power of Elijah to turn the hearts of fathers toward children and ... to prepare a people fit for the Lord" (Lk 1:17).

John the Baptist's mission, like Elijah's, involves healing family relationships. Our society today sorely needs such healing. Many people have been deeply hurt in various ways by other family members. Jesus took all of that pain and nailed it to the cross. We can unite our pain to his and he will heal us of our wounds. We can confess whatever ways we may have hurt others. Saint Paul says, "And you who once were alienated … he has now reconciled in his fleshly body through his death, to present you holy, without blemish, and irreproachable before him …" (Col 1:21–22).

Is there some relationship in your life that needs healing and reconciliation? Ask the Lord to give you the healing you desire. Even if the other person cannot or will not respond, Jesus can remove the pain from your heart. Our peace of mind does not depend on the attitudes that other people hold toward us. It depends only on what the Lord is doing in us. And he always brings grace.

Oratio

Lord Jesus, I ask you for the grace of healing in my life. Restore broken relationships, especially the ones in which I have suffered the most pain. Forgive me, too, for any ways in which I may have hurt other persons. If I am still clinging to any resentment or bitterness, help me to let go of it and to forgive. Bring peace and joy to my family, so that together we may celebrate your coming at Christmas with love and reconciliation.

Contemplatio

"Then the disciples understood."

Sunday of the Third Week of Advent — A

∴ · · · · · · · · · · · ∴

Lectio

Matthew 11:2–11

Meditatio

"... in prison ..."

This Gospel passage has often intrigued me. John is "in prison," yet the Gospel says that he recognizes the works of the Messiah. The Gospel also tells us that John sends his disciples to Jesus to ask him if he is the one they are waiting for—the Messiah—or if they should wait for another. It sounds as if John isn't sure whether Jesus is the Messiah. I have often wanted to ask John, "What happened?" When Jesus came to John to be baptized, John tried to prevent him. He said that Jesus should baptize him instead (Mt 3:14). What has happened to John to cause him to question Jesus' authenticity?

Nothing. It isn't that John doubts Jesus' status as Messiah. John remains the precursor to the Incarnate Word. John is doing what he has always done, what we are all called to do: pointing to the Messiah. Although John is physically imprisoned, it is his disciples who are in a kind of prison from which only Jesus can free them. It is a prison of their pre-conceived ideas, a prison maybe even of their fear of the unknown. John knows the truth of the Messiah and is free because he continues to do what God is asking him to do. But John wishes to release his disciples from their imprisonment.

Sometimes people have a hard time taking other people's word for something. John invites his disciples to ask this question about Jesus as Messiah, knowing full well that Jesus will quench their thirst for the truth. And what does Jesus do? How does he free them? He invites them to really see and hear; he invites them to become witnesses and then sends them to witness. It is in seeing and hearing that they come to believe, and it is in witnessing that they come to full freedom as children of God.

Oratio

O Jesus, Messiah, certain ideas, fears, and anxieties imprison me and keep me from witnessing to your marvelous works in the world in general and in my world in particular. You became man so that we can be truly free, so that we can recognize the gift of being called God's sons and daughters. Open my eyes and ears, Lord, to see and hear all you are doing and all the ways you are blessing me this day. Help me to be a faith-filled witness in the full freedom God has given me.

Contemplatio

"Go and tell ... what you hear and see...."

Sunday of the Third Week of Advent — B

∴ .... ∴

Lectio

John 1:6–8; 19–28

Meditatio

"Who are you?"

"So, what's your story?" someone who wants to get to know you might ask after the usual polite questions, "What's your name?" and "What do you do?" The question "Who are you?" goes deeper.

Priests and Levites were sent to ask John the Baptist: "Who are you?" John's life both intrigued and challenged those around him. His first answer is telling: "I am not the Messiah." He's not pretending to be who he's not. Borrowing from the prophet Isaiah, John defines himself as "the voice of one crying out in the desert, 'Make straight the way of the LORD'" (see Is 40:3). John's life centers on the Lord.

In our life's journey, God wants us to fully claim who we are. He came that we might have life, abundant life. John's testimony is not about denying his reality as a person created and loved by God. Instead, John recognizes the unique mission God has entrusted to him, and John accepts his identity as one called to point to the Messiah. What is our identity?

Part of knowing who we are involves knowing where we have come from. In the realm of the Spirit, knowing *whose* we are is essential. Who or what claims my heart? What do I know of my Creator? What is my relationship with God?

In another passage, Jesus asks his disciples: "Who do you say that I am?" (see Mt 16:15). During the remaining days of Advent, ask the Lord to reveal to you more fully who God is and wants to be for you. Saint Augustine believed that the more you know of God, the more you know of yourself. Like parent, like child. It works the other way around too. It's part of being made in the image and likeness of God (see Gen 1)!

Oratio

Lord, you called me into being out of love. You made me in your image and likeness. I am a marvel of your creation! As you did for John the Baptist, reveal to me the plan you have dreamed for my life. Continue to reveal yourself to me that my life may be a response to your creative love. Each day, as I look forward to a new manifestation of your presence, may I further claim my filial relationship to you. May those whom I encounter see the resemblance between us. Lord, come and be born in my heart each day! I want to proclaim you through my life. Amen.

Contemplatio

I am God's precious child.

Sunday of the Third Week of Advent — C

∴ ············ ∴

Lectio

Luke 3:10–18

Meditatio

>*"[W]hat should we do?"*

In today's Gospel many types of people surround John the Baptist—simple workers, tax collectors, and even soldiers. John's message of repentance moves them interiorly and draws them all together, but each group needs special coaching on how to follow the Lord. So they asked John, "What should we do?"

A coach can size us up, look at how we're playing the game, and assess our strengths and our weaknesses. No matter what the skill, art, or game, a coach can help us reach an excellence we could never achieve on our own. John the Baptist, a good coach, takes the individuals in that crowd where they are and challenges them to grow.

Although John could point out the areas where they need conversion, he cannot give them the strength to actually change their lives. Yet that is what the people want. They not only wanted John to tell them what they should do, but they also longed for the one who could make inner conversion possible.

This is truly a story about grace—God mysteriously and secretly working in the hearts of these people. The crowd senses God's presence as they cry out for help to change their lives. But God is working so secretly within them and around them that the people begin to wonder whether John himself is the Christ. Hope fills their hearts with expectation for the one who could give them the inner strength to live new lives. Like a good coach, John assures them that they were longing for another, for the one who would baptize with the Holy Spirit and fire.

Hearing the call to conversion is a beautiful and painful experience. Beauty comes through the grace God fills us with, which calls us to let go of sin and darkness and to live more fully. Pain comes through our own weakness and inability to change. But God meets us here in a profound way. He gives us the inner strength to make these changes. All we have to do is ask!

Oratio

Jesus, I hear your call to look more closely at my life and to see the ways I can love more and die to myself. Thank you for this grace. I want to change and grow and love, Lord, but I don't know how. You have to show me.

As I pray these words, I know that you are already here, ready and waiting to walk with me.

Contemplatio

"[T]he people were filled with expectation."

Monday of the Third Week of Advent[*]

∴ ⋯⋯⋯⋯ ∴

Lectio

Matthew 21:23–27

Meditatio

> *"By what authority are you doing these things?"*

Take a moment to imagine the scene. Jesus has just entered triumphantly into Jerusalem, drawing a large crowd who treat him as royalty. Then he immediately goes to the Temple. But he does not go as a visitor; he goes as one in authority! He upsets the whole system, driving out all those who were buying and selling. Jesus overturns tables and welcomes in the blind and the lame! He ignores custom and shows a blatant disregard for the authority of the chief priests, who have ruled the Temple for years.

Is it any wonder that in today's Gospel, the chief priests have arrived on the scene to question Jesus? In a real sense, they are asking, "Who do you think you are?"

Because we know the end of the story, we may be quick to judge the chief priests for their lack of faith and their effort to ensnare Jesus. But if we were living then, where would we find ourselves? Would we be among the poor, the

---

[*] For Advent reflections from December 17 to December 24, see pp. 66–81.

lame, and the blind following after the Christ, a simple man from the Galilean countryside? Or would we be among those scandalized by his unruly behavior and failure to obey custom, by his unspoken claim to be the anointed one of God?

Sometimes we may forget that Jesus was not tame. He disregarded the social order and upset people's expectations. He spoke the truth and acted from it even when it gained him nothing but the anger and ill will of those who felt they had a better claim to authority. It would do us well to remember that in the end, this cost him his life.

But Jesus never forgot who he was and where his authority came from. By recalling the baptism of John the Baptist, he gives a hint as to the source of his authority. This reminds us of Jesus' own baptism where he was anointed by the Holy Spirit, and where was heard the voice from Heaven: "This is my beloved Son."

Oratio

Lord Jesus, you have set an example for me to follow. With you, I am called and sent through my baptism to preach and to live the truth, even when to do so may only be done at a cost. This leaves me to question myself: Has my living of the Christian life become too comfortable? As I walk with you this Advent, help me to be open to the ways you may be challenging me to stand up for truth. Give me the courage to defend all that is of you—all that is holy, good, and true.

Contemplatio

"This is my beloved Son. Listen to him" (Mk 9:7).

Tuesday of the Third Week of Advent[*]

∵ ·········· ∴

Lectio

Matthew 21:28–32

Meditatio

> *"[T]ax collectors and prostitutes
> are entering the kingdom of God before you."*

I used to take this little parable of the two sons and the vineyard literally: It's better to say "no" and obey than to say "yes" and disobey. Later, I understood that it's best to say "yes" and to live what I say! Later still, I noticed the punch line, in which Jesus says that the marginalized are entering God's kingdom before the self-righteous.

And so, I wonder ...

Where do I stand? Am I living as a follower of Jesus or am I only kidding myself? Do I view society's marginalized as people about whom God cares deeply? How do I regard and treat relatives, neighbors, or acquaintances whose lifestyles and priorities are different from my own? Do I accept them?

I may find that some of society's marginalized take more interest in religion and show more loving concern for others

[*] For Advent reflections from December 17 to December 24, see pp. 66–81.

than some pillars of the Church do. If this doesn't seem true from my experience, I can wonder: Who's at fault? Perhaps I am. Perhaps I've alienated these persons instead of showing them the acceptance and love that Jesus showed to the marginalized around him. As a Catholic and a Christian, I'm supposed to be a Christ-bearer, but have I truly let the Lord reach out to his poor ones through me?

What changes do I need to make to become more like Jesus? Whom do I need to include among my friends and associates? How can I reach out to the alienated and marginalized in my workplace, neighborhood, or family? How can I show Christ's compassionate love to them?

This is the "acceptable time," the "day of salvation" (2 Cor 6:2). What will I do? When and how will I do it?

Oratio

Lord Jesus, help me to offer to others the love and acceptance that you yourself extended to the marginalized and alienated. Help me to see how today's marginalized are like the men and women with whom you chose to associate during your ministry. May I look beyond external actions and see people for whom you have great dreams—persons whom you want to call closer to yourself through my presence, actions, or words. Help me to let you speak and act through me, so they will truly experience your love for them. I ask these graces from the Father in your name.

Contemplatio

"Which of the two did his father's will?"

Wednesday of the Third Week of Advent*

⸭ ··········· ⸭

Lectio

Luke 7:18b–23

Meditatio

> *"Are you the one who is to come,*
> *or should we look for another?"*

John has been hearing about the teachings and wonders attributed to Jesus: Jesus had chosen a group of disciples; he taught multitudes about the blessed life, about the love of enemies and the power of forgiveness; he had cured the servant of a centurion, raised a widow's son. People flocked to him hoping just to touch him "because power came forth from him and healed them all" (Lk 6:19). All this made John's heart race. Jesus had come to him for baptism, and he had been moved to prophesy about Jesus. He remembers well those words that came spontaneously to his lips, "[O]ne mightier than I is coming. I am not worthy to loosen the thongs of his sandals. He will baptize you with the holy Spirit and fire" (Lk 3:16).

---

* For Advent reflections from December 17 to December 24, see pp. 66–81.

Now John's followers are confused. "What does all this mean? Should we leave you and follow this other teacher?" they ask. The answer was clear to John, but they must hear it directly from Jesus. When they approach and ask if he is the One, Jesus' reply is not only for them, but also for all disciples down through the ages. "Don't the message and the miracles speak for themselves? John can interpret this for you." John's disciples were blessed in that they actually saw Jesus and heard his voice. But we are blessed because we can reach back into the Church's memory and join that scene. This Advent day we are drawn into that wonderful dialogue between Jesus and John's followers. We see their dilemma. We watch John nudge them toward Jesus. We come with them to Jesus and taste the excitement that surrounds him. He says to them and to us: "Go and tell John what you have seen and heard."

Oratio

Lord, make me as John the Baptist to the people who surround me. Although in my heart I want others to appreciate me and listen to my every word, let me direct them to you. In you are found consolation, strength, healing, and hope. Give me an Advent heart that finds its joy in pointing out the Way to others.

Contemplatio

"Go and tell John what you have seen and heard."

Thursday of the Third Week of Advent[*]

⁚ · · · · · · · · · · · ⁚

Lectio

Luke 7:24–30

Meditatio

> *"I tell you, among those born of women,*
> *no one is greater than John...."*

King Herod put John the Baptist in prison because he spoke the truth. When Jesus speaks to the crowds about John, he first refers to images of what John is not—a reed that sways in the wind, someone dressed in fine clothes. Ironically these characteristics describe Herod, who lived for a luxurious life, had no moral backbone, and let his fears get the best of him. Amazingly, Jesus said that John was the greatest among those born of woman, of every human who had ever lived.

Many in Israel had forgotten the love that God had for them as his people, and they disregarded their responsibilities to him. John's vocation was to prepare the way of the Lord; prepare the hearts of all so they could receive and welcome their promised Messiah. John never seeks anything for his own glory, recognizing that he is only God's servant. He realizes that some would not only reject his bold message but

---

[*] For Advent reflections from December 17 to December 24, see pp. 66–81.

that they would also, as happened to prophets before him, persecute him. He has prepared himself to be a faithful herald, an unbending prophet, by living an austere life in the desert. It is a barren place with no comforts, far from the lure of an easy life, where only the strong can survive. John listens to God's word and is docile to the promptings of the Spirit in the desert, where God can more easily speak to his heart.

It is easy to lose sight of Advent's purpose by focusing only on our preparations of gifts and parties for others. Advent is an opportunity to accept God's plan for us by preparing ourselves to welcome Christ into our hearts. John gives us an example of how to reflect on God's word while he also challenges us to change our lives by rejecting temptation.

Oratio

Jesus, make me as docile to you as was John the Baptist, who recognized that he was a messenger of God, a precursor and not the Messiah. I'm afraid that desire for human esteem and a comfortable life may block my ability to follow you today. Through John's intercession, may I show in my words and actions that you are the Lord of my life. May I act to help others prepare their minds and hearts to receive and welcome you into their lives. Let your first coming not be in vain in our lives, but be accepted and corresponded to, so that we will be ready for your second coming.

Contemplatio

O God, may I always listen to your word with a welcoming heart.

Friday of the Third Week of Advent[*]

:• ·········· •:

Lectio

John 5:33–36

Meditatio

"[T]hese works that I perform testify ... that the Father has sent me."

In TV courtroom dramas, the turning point often comes when the prosecutor asks a witness, "Could you please identify that person for the jury?" The moment of truth arrives.

The Gospel for this Advent Friday is proclaimed in the liturgy only rarely, when Advent begins in November and December 16 falls on a Friday. So we seldom experience this forensic scene in which Jesus is presenting a new witness for the defense (or is it the prosecution?).

The first witness has already been summoned: John the Baptist. Jesus does not dismiss John's testimony. In fact, he says that John was a "burning and shining lamp": high praise from the "Light of the World" (cf. Jn 9:5)!

Superficial qualities such as fame, wealth, or talent can become the standards by which other people (or ourselves) are routinely judged. In calling his next witness, Jesus is asking us to use better judgment. He warns us of a cult of

---

[*] For Advent reflections from December 17 to December 24, see pp. 66–81.

celebrity that would give more weight to John's picturesque testimony than to the works of the Father. Those "works" are the witness Jesus calls to the stand. Jesus doesn't claim anything as his own: he keeps referring all his miracles (his "signs" in the Gospel's vocabulary) to the Father. Those works are the Father's presence and action that have come among us in Jesus. The works themselves testify to the meaning and message of Christmas: God is with us in Jesus!

The center of this section of John's Gospel declares, "John testified to the truth" (cf. Jn 5:33). More than a lamp, John is a spotlight, drawing people's gaze to the One whom an ancient Christian hymn calls "the brightness of the Father's glory." Now, Saint Paul will say, it is we who are called to be "light in the Lord" (Eph 5:8). "The works I do," Jesus says, "you shall do, and greater far than these" (cf. Jn 14:12).

Oratio

Lord Jesus, thank you for blessing me with your Gospel. The Father gave you works to accomplish, and you share your mission with me. You said you could do nothing on your own, apart from the Father. How much more do I need to remain in communion with you so that my choices, my words, my works will bear witness to you! In my daily routine, in my work, among my family, neighbors, and co-workers, I want to testify to the truth that God is still at work, making all things come together for good.

Contemplatio

Brightness of the Father's glory, shine upon us!

Sunday of the Fourth Week of Advent — A

⁖ ⋯⋯⋯⋯ ⁖

Lectio

Matthew 1:18–24

Meditatio

> *"When Joseph awoke, he did as the angel of the Lord*
> *had commanded him...."*

I can just imagine Joseph lying awake at night. The woman he wants to marry is suddenly, obviously, with child. Mary had been away to visit her cousin Elizabeth and had returned with no explanation for her pregnancy. How could she have done this to him? What should he do? He loves her. He does not want to see her hurt. Night after sleepless night he searches the heavens for an answer.

We also find ourselves at times in perplexing, heartbreaking situations that involve people we love and trust. In this narrative about Joseph, we find the steps for dealing with our perplexity and mending our hearts.

First, Joseph acts with integrity in searching for God's guidance in a seemingly no-win situation. He decides to divorce Mary quietly. It would be the best for them. He seeks God's direction with a certain calmness. The angry grinding of our minds over the injustices we see brought against us can keep us awake at night. Joseph is at peace in his search.

The angel sheds the light of God's direction on Joseph's situation. We can discover God's intent through meditating on the Scriptures, consulting Church teachings, pondering the deeper meaning of events, seeking the guidance of a holy person. God will often ask us to do things that don't make complete sense. He tells Joseph to marry a pregnant virgin because the child is from the Holy Spirit. That must have been as clear as mud to Joseph. He must have been used to experiencing God's guidance to have immediately recognized God's voice as he did. A certain type of peace comes when one deeply understands the ways of God, even when what the Lord commands is perplexing or unexpected. This experience comes from the habit of referring all our needs and decisions to the Lord.

Finally Joseph wakes and does what he has been told to do. In the face of ridicule and marginalization, Joseph obeys. What a marvelous horizon opens up to him and all of us as a result—much more expansive than to "divorce her quietly."

Oratio

Lord, I place the decisions I need to make and the problems I need to solve into your hands. Guide me, and I will trust you.

Contemplatio

Guide me, Lord, and I will trust you.

Sunday of the Fourth Week of Advent — B

∴ ⋯⋯⋯⋯ ∴

Lectio

Luke 1:26–38

Meditatio

> *"… the Lord God will give him the throne of David his father,*
> *and he will rule over the house of Jacob forever,*
> *and of his kingdom there will be no end."*

Sometimes it seems God's promises lay dormant for a long time! Who has not waited for good things to happen to our loved ones after months or years of prayer? The Annunciation to the Virgin Mary is a much-cherished story of how God fulfills his promises in ways and at times that exceed what we could ever imagine! The Father always manifests himself and acts through his Son and the Holy Spirit.

It took almost a thousand years for God's promises to David to find their fulfillment in Jesus. No one could have predicted the marvelous way God's providential plan would reveal itself! Instead of an earthly king, the Father sends his Son through the "yes" of a modest virgin living in an insignificant town of a conquered people. God sends a King far beyond anyone's expectations or dreams, his own Son who embraces our human condition.

In this lovely reading, we hear again of Israel's ancient longing fulfilled in Mary's "yes," and of God's goodness to Elizabeth who conceives her long-desired child. God fulfills his promises to these holy women in ways that surpassed their deepest hopes and expectations!

Have you ever experienced a disappointment that broke your heart, with little hope for the future? If you are patient and wait for God's time, God will give you something much more precious. Perhaps you found that such a purification brought you to a deeper intimacy with God in prayer and to an inner freedom. What we learn during this journey of disappointment, purification, and trust often leads us to say, "I wouldn't choose to experience that kind of disappointment again, but neither would I exchange what I have learned about myself and God's goodness for anything! God's dream for me was so much bigger than I ever imagined!"

Oratio

Jesus, the "fullness of time" (cf. Gal 4:4) arrived for us at the moment of the Incarnation when you embraced our humanity in the womb of the Virgin Mary. Your love for me is always more than I can imagine. You give me what I need when I need it. May your Spirit help me today to recognize and welcome the people through whom you are acting in my life. Help me to trust in your tender providence and to surrender to your plan of love. You know what is best!

Contemplatio

"May it be done to me according to your word."

Sunday of the Fourth Week of Advent — C

⠒ ⠄⠄⠄⠄⠄⠄⠄⠄⠄⠄ ⠴

Lectio

> Luke 1:39–45

Meditatio

> *"For at the moment the sound of your greeting reached my ears,*
> *the infant in my womb leaped for joy."*

One of the time-honored titles for Mary is *Cause of Our Joy.* Do you know anyone who has been a cause of joy to you? Someone who lights up your day just by being present? Someone who always seems to have a kind word and who leaves your heart feeling lighter? Mary is like that. When we let her into our life as disciples of her Son, she brings joy and peace to our hearts. And she never comes alone. She always brings Jesus.

The Gospel tells us that Mary went "in haste" to visit Elizabeth. She knew that the older woman was approaching the last part of her pregnancy and would need help. So without thinking about her own needs, Mary hurries to help Elizabeth. Could we possibly think Mary is any different now? No! In heaven she intercedes for us, and she still hurries to help us in all of our needs.

In these final days before Christmas, it's easy to get swept into hectic last-minute shopping, parties, and errands. These can take our focus away from Jesus. In the midst of all the chaos, take just a few minutes and spend them quietly with Mary. Close your eyes, breathe quietly, focusing on your heart, and imagine that Mary is there with you. Just feel grateful for her presence, for coming to you, for bringing us Jesus. Ask her to show you how you can bring joy to others, just as she did throughout her life on earth. Then listen. Mary will whisper the answer in your heart. Like Elizabeth, we might ask, "And how does this happen to me, that the mother of my Lord should come to me?" It happens because Mary cares about us.

Oratio

Mary, my Mother, I turn to you with great trust, and I ask you for the help I need right now. You who are the *Cause of Our Joy*, come and bring joy and peace into my life and the lives of all my loved ones. Teach me to act as you did, to be attentive to the needs of others, and to be willing to give of myself. In everything I do, may I be a mirror that reflects the image of your Son, Jesus.

Contemplatio

"And how does this happen to me, that the mother of my Lord should come to me?"

December 17

∴ ⋯⋯⋯ ∴

Lectio

Matthew 1:1–17

Meditatio

> *"Of her was born Jesus who is called the Messiah."*

At first, these verses may simply seem to be a collection of names and therefore incapable of producing meaning. However, these verses, like Mary, are pregnant with hidden treasure. The list of names produces a pattern that creates an expectation. It becomes predictable. One man fathers another; one generation follows another; after every fourteen generations an event important to the history of the Chosen People takes place.

This pattern is randomly broken with the inclusion of several women whose marital status or ethnicity is outside of the norm. They are the key that unlocks the passage's meaning. The Chosen People's expectation is shattered. The Messiah, the Son of David, is not fathered. Rather, his sole human origin lies in a woman. Whose son is he? Whose name does he bear? Whose inheritance can he claim?

And what about the fourteen generations? Each set of fourteen generations is made up of two sets of seven generations. So, six sets of generations have preceded Jesus. His generation inaugurates the seventh set and ushers in the Jubilee Year (see Lev 25:8–11). In the Jubilee Year all were supposed to return to their "ancestral property," thus reclaiming their patrimony. For those generations following the period of exile, the significance of the Jubilee Year— returning home—would have had tremendous meaning.

Jesus is the brother who redeems us and restores us to the family of God (see Lev 25:35–55). And since he inaugurates the Jubilee Generation, we are also set free to reclaim the inheritance that was lost through original sin. This Jubilee Generation has no end.

Oratio

Father of all, Father of Jesus, our Father, my Father.

I experience in many ways the consequences of sin. My expectations are often based on the repetition of patterns rather than on your promise. Break the patterns in my life that hold me bound in servitude. Allow me to recognize that when patterns are broken in my life, you are drawing near to be with me. Help me to welcome the freedom you offer me through your Son, my brother—a freedom that restores our relationship. You are my Father; I am your child. Amen.

Contemplatio

"I will be a father to him, and he shall be a son to me … I will maintain him in my house and in my kingdom forever …" (1 Chr 17:13–14).

December 18

.: ·········· .:

Lectio

Matthew 1:18–25

Meditatio

> *"[Y]ou are to name him Jesus. . . ."*

In his first chapter Matthew goes to great lengths to relate the human ancestry of . . . Jesus? No, of Joseph, the husband of Mary, to whom was born Jesus the Christ. Through the angel, Joseph is asked to become Jesus' legal father. And by naming the child, Joseph complies with God's request. Jesus becomes "Son of David."

This is another of God's marvelous interventions in human history. Sarah, Hannah, and Mary's cousin Elizabeth all conceived sons when conception seemed impossible. Gideon routed the Midianites with only a few hundred men. Samson performed feats of extraordinary strength. The Maccabees fought against overwhelming odds to overthrow the Seleucids. And now, here again, God is entering perceptibly into human events. He is becoming present in an entirely new way.

Yet the Lord is always present! He cares about his sons and daughters! His interventions in our lives are usually cloaked in ordinary events, but they are real nonetheless.

Have we ever marveled when a difficult situation was unexpectedly resolved? Have we ever felt gently chided: "O you of little faith, why did you doubt?" (see Mt 14:31). As Saint Paul says, when we're in difficulty and temptation, God will give us a way out (see 1 Cor 10:13). Each of us may remember some examples of this in our own lives. "If God is for us," asks Paul, "who can be against us?" (Rom 8:31).

Now, one week before Christmas, we might continue reflecting with Paul on what our Father has done for us: "God sent his Son, born of a woman" (Gal 4:4); "He who did not spare his own Son but handed him over for us all, how will he not give us everything else along with him?" (Rom 8:32).

Yes! Emmanuel is coming—God with us! Let us prepare our hearts to welcome him.

Oratio

Father in heaven, you sent your Son into the world to be our brother, companion, and Savior. In him your ever-present love for us became visible, and we recognize your care and concern for each of us. Help us to be grateful always that Jesus came into the world as one of us. May we trust firmly in your providence, especially when life becomes difficult and seems to lose meaning, joy, or peace. May we place our hopes in your Son and trust that he is with us, sharing our burdens, our sorrows, our joys.

Contemplatio

"They shall name him Emmanuel."

December 19

∴ · · · · · · · · · · · ∴

Lectio

Luke 1:5–25

Meditatio

> *"[Y]ou will be speechless…."*

When people say, "I'm speechless!" they are usually reacting with awe and amazement to some good thing that has surprised them. The event may also evoke feelings of gratitude, humility, and wonder.

Gratitude and wonder would have been a proper response of Zechariah to the angel Gabriel's announcement. Instead, Zechariah replies, "How shall I know this?" Compared with Mary's response to the same angel, Zechariah's at first seems similar. Mary says, "How can this be?" However, Mary's question does not doubt the reality but only asks for information about means and ways. Zechariah asks for something to verify that what is said will come to pass. "How [literally, by what] shall I know this?" could be loosely translated, "Prove it to me." Zechariah wants a sign that will convince him to put his trust in the good news communicated by the angel.

Do we sometimes respond in a similar way to the promises of God's action in our lives? It's almost as if we fear to trust and hope, lest we be disappointed or find out we have been deceived. One senses this is Zechariah's response—that what Gabriel says is too good to be true. And no wonder! At his age, having a son is impossible, humanly speaking. His wife, Elizabeth, had never been able to have a child and is now past child-bearing age. So how can he now hope for a child? No doubt he let go of such hopes a long time ago, as he and his wife, Elizabeth, grew older.

So, because Zechariah has not reacted with figurative speechlessness, the angel inflicts literal speechlessness on him: he will be mute until the announced good news comes to pass. Thus, he gets his sign and the amazing pregnancy of Elizabeth occurs, followed by the birth of a son to an old man who had long since stopped hoping for such a gift.

Oratio

Jesus, help me learn from the experience of Zechariah the kind of attitude I should have in the face of your promises and action in my life—speechlessness at seeing your grace at work in me and in the world. Help me always to trust, not doubt, and to let my soul fill with wonder and expectation, not a jaded suspicion. Nothing is impossible for you.

Contemplatio

You are amazing, Lord.

December 20

⁞ · · · · · · · · · · · · ⁞

Lectio

Luke 1:26–38

Meditatio

"Do not be afraid, Mary, for you have found favor with God."

The liturgy focuses on Mary today, as the birth of Jesus approaches quickly. Years ago, this Mass was called the "Golden Mass," and was celebrated with special solemnity. Sometimes, in the Middle Ages, the Annunciation scene was even acted out. The liturgy is simpler today. But it still draws us into the mystery of Mary and the angel Gabriel.

Silence falls over us as we contemplate that scene. We don't want to intrude on Mary's privacy. What was she doing when the angel came? Praying, perhaps? Or was she working, busy at spinning or sewing or cooking? Recently I saw a painting of the Annunciation that intrigued me. Mary is shown from behind, as she slowly walks toward a point of light at the other end of an empty room.

However it happened, the greatest event of human history came quietly, without fanfare. Everyone knew that the really important events were happening in Rome, where Augustus Caesar was forging an empire. Who cared about a simple peasant girl and her baby?

But through that young girl, the Incarnation happened. Mary gave us Jesus, our Savior, our Redeemer, our Way, our Truth, our Life. The Incarnation was the greatest event in human history. And at the time no one but Mary knew it had even happened.

Now we are only five days away from Christmas. God offers each of us an invitation, just as he offered one to Mary. It comes in secret, just for you. No one else knows. Pause for a moment. Take a few moments for prayer, even in this busy season. Ask your heart, not your head; "What is God inviting me to this Christmas?"

The liturgy makes present the grace of the mysteries it celebrates. We do not just remember an event that happened long ago as if we were reading a history book. Through the liturgy, God comes to speak to us, to make a proposal, to offer us his love, just as he offered Mary an invitation.

Oratio

Mary, my Mother, I thank you for saying "yes" to God's invitation to become the Mother of his Son. Your heart was ready for this grace, because you always wanted to do God's will in everything. Help me, too, as I struggle in my life, to accept the invitations God is sending me. Help me to respond just as you did, with your joyful "yes" that does not consider the cost. "Hail, favored one! The Lord is with you!"

Contemplatio

"Behold, I am the handmaid of the Lord. May it be done to me according to your word."

December 21

✦ ············ ✦

Lectio

Luke 1:39–45

Meditatio

"… for joy …"

Christmas is just a few days away. Most of us still have lots of things to do as we prepare for our liturgies and our family celebrations. And so, today's Gospel is especially for us. We find echoes of the pre-holiday hustle and bustle in Mary's hasty journey through the difficult hill country.

Mary was very young, pregnant, and certainly preoccupied with her own future. For these reasons we are moved by her thoughtfulness, concern, and care every time we read this passage. In announcing to her God's plans, the Archangel Gabriel tells her, as a means of reassuring her, that her older, barren cousin is also with child. Mary goes quickly to Elizabeth, eager to serve.

We expect exuberance from the young. It is one of life's delights. Luke recreates this delight in the heart of today's Advent saint, Elizabeth. We are not told the words or manner of Mary's greeting to Elizabeth, but we can imagine how it must have been by Elizabeth's reaction; "The moment the sound of your greeting reached my ears, the infant in my womb leaped for joy." At that moment of encounter, the Holy Spirit has filled the older woman's heart and she cries out an astonished blessing. How could she have known Mary's own sweet secret? From where does her prophetic praise arise? How does she know the young girl has brought the Promised One to her humble home?

As we prepare to celebrate Christmas this year, let us return to this scene and imagine the days that followed and try to feel the joy that must have dwelt in every little word and gesture these holy women shared. As the day of Christ's coming nears, let our hearts leap and our voices cry out in joy.

Oratio

Lord, I address this prayer to your Mother knowing the joy that gives you. Mary, reflecting on your journey and the meeting that took place between you and Elizabeth is to me a portrait of grace. You illustrate the gentle yet exuberant approach of God's grace to my soul and in Elizabeth I see the soul's astounded but joyful reception. May you, the Mother full of grace, make me a kind and joyful person, willing to serve unselfishly.

Contemplatio

"Blessed are you who believed that what was spoken to you by the Lord would be fulfilled."

December 22

⁑ ·········· ⁑

Lectio

Luke 1:46–56

Meditatio

> *"My soul proclaims the greatness of the Lord...."*

These words from Luke resonate so well with our hopes and desires. They express the universal experience encountered by one who has met the Lord. Mary begins, "My soul proclaims the greatness of the Lord...." And every line that follows echoes this proclamation. It is a song about the Lord, not about her, as her life is about the Lord.

We too can pray these words from the depths of our soul as Mary does. When God becomes the center of our lives, when we recognize God as the protagonist, the Giver of all we have, and Provider for our every need, we too can step aside to let him lead us. Then we spontaneously praise God for such undeserved and abundant care.

With faith to guide us, each of us could write a unique magnificat. How has the Lord blessed me? Let me proclaim the ways! I too can recognize that I am a "lowly servant," one who doesn't count for much in the eyes of society, but that God has looked upon me with favor and become my Savior. As I look back on my life with the eyes of faith and consider my life today, I can rejoice that whatever my need, God has been there to provide for me. God will always be there.

As I look back in faith, I see that God has shown me mercy in the many times I have received healing through the sacrament of Penance, in the good health and other blessings I and my loved ones have received, in the opportunities for growth through the painful events of life.

God has been at work even in circumstances that allowed me to be "thrown down" or when I was "arrogant of mind and heart." But I have always been "lifted up" anew. When I have been self-satisfied, God has allowed me to lack the affirmation or applause I would have liked. Instead, when I willingly allow others to shine, the Lord provides without hesitation.

Oratio

Lord God, help me to see only and always with the eyes of faith. You are at work in my life, in the lives of my loved ones, and in every circumstance I encounter. Help me to trust that you will always bring good out of each moment, even if I am presently unable to see it. Help me to believe that your love for me is far more powerful than anything I may encounter.

Mary, you who recognized God's goodness even in your most difficult sufferings, help me to believe with your faith.

Contemplatio

Lord, at all times and in every circumstance may I proclaim your greatness.

December 23

∴ ⋯⋯⋯ ∴

Lectio

Luke 1:57–66

Meditatio

"What, then, will this child be?"

As each of my nieces and nephews was born (and especially when I had a chance to see them soon after birth), a feeling of awe and wonder struck me. What a little bundle of potential a newborn baby is! Each child is a mystery. What will he become? What will she be like?

We can spot some clues—long feet and toes indicating future height, for example. We can surmise some likely possibilities—the prospect of inheriting gifts and inclinations from artistic, athletic, or musically gifted parents, for instance. But no one except God can know for sure anything about the future deeds, accomplishments, influence, or lifespan of the child. And only a foolish person would claim to know the future.

A child like John, the son of Elizabeth and Zechariah, is the focus of wonder because each child is a gift from God to the world—a sign that God has not finished with us yet.

The extraordinary circumstances around John's birth make people take notice. Obviously, God is involved because this baby would not even have been conceived in the normal way of things. But God is involved in each child's life, and indeed each person's, no matter at what stage of life, no matter what a person may have done or not done previously. Every human being has marvelous potential and is a mystery known only to God.

Sometimes we sell each other and ourselves short. We might look at a person or at ourselves and feel that our future paths are already laid out. That is not true. God always provides the grace needed to change. We can always change direction or focus, or deepen our commitment, or repent of our selfishness, and allow God to transform us. The Baby born in Bethlehem reminds us of this.

Oratio

God, my Father, thank you for the gift that every single child is to the world. Thank you for the renewal of wonder, awe, and hope that every baby brings. Is that why your Son came as a baby—to awaken in people a new hope in your grace at work in the world?

I am a mystery of your grace. Thank you for the gift of being able to begin again. Help me never to despair of the possibility of change, either in myself or in those around me.

Contemplatio

What will you do in me today, Lord?

December 24 — Mass in the Morning

⁘ · · · · · · · · · · · ⁖

Lectio

Luke 1:67–79

Meditatio

> *"… the daybreak from on high will visit us…."*

This promised daybreak is the One whose birth we celebrate tomorrow. More than two thousand years ago he came to shine on those who lived in darkness. He brought hope and healing and forgiveness of sins. He died out of love for us, and he destroyed the finality of death by his resurrection. He sent his followers to continue his mission, and he said he would be with them until the end of the world.

So … why do we still dwell "in the shadow of death"? Why are we not on the "way of peace," but instead are on the way of war, confusion, and hatred? Why have we not yet been set free of all this?

Yes, the dawn has broken, but we do not yet enjoy the full light of day. The Incarnation ended the night, but the complete fulfillment of the promise will occur only when Jesus comes again at the end of the world. (The name of the liturgical season that ends today—Advent—means "coming." It refers to both comings of Jesus—his first coming as a baby, and his final coming at the world's end.)

In apostolic times, believers ardently looked forward to Jesus' coming again. From them we have the acclamation, "*Maranatha!*," which means, "Come, Lord!" They seem to have thought that the parousia, the second coming, would happen very soon, most likely within their lifetimes.

Over the centuries, as the parousia has not occurred, we have lost much of the expectation and longing the first Christians had. We certainly look askance at those who say they expect the coming of Jesus in their lifetime. But why? Maybe we need some reminders that this world is not all there is. Jesus will come again, and then he will establish endless day!

Oratio

Jesus, I wasn't there for your first coming, and I have no idea when your final coming will be. But every day you come to me in so many ways. You speak to me in the Scriptures, in prayer, through the kindness of others, and in the opportunities for doing good that are your gift to me. You come to me in the sacrament of Reconciliation and in Holy Communion. Help me renew my expectation for these comings, so that I am always on the watch for you everywhere.

Contemplatio

Maranatha! Come Lord Jesus!

On a cold winter's night
the Son of God is born
in a hidden stable
where animals lodge ...

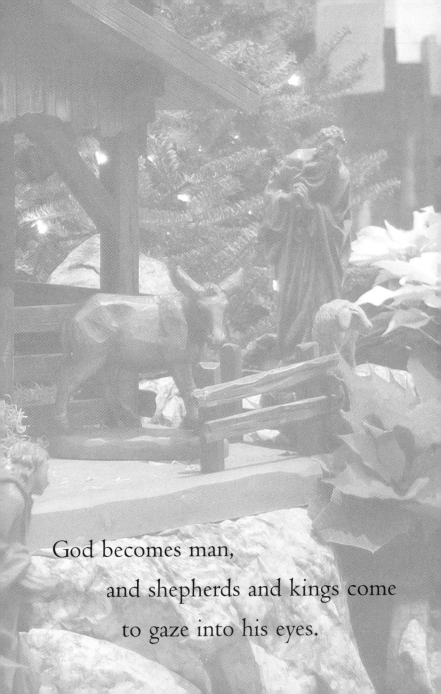

God becomes man,

and shepherds and kings come

to gaze into his eyes.

December 25 — Christmas Midnight Mass

∴ ·········· ∵

Lectio

Luke 2:1–14

Meditatio

"She wrapped him in swaddling clothes...."

Every mother and father knows that it's not a newborn's "swaddling clothes" that consume a parent's attention. Rather, it's the child's eyes, the shape of the nose, the color of the hair, the dimple just like grandmother's, the smile. We are drawn to contemplate the baby's face.

Jesus' birth surprises us with the first look at God's face! For the Chosen People no one could look on the face of God and live. Even the thought of seeing God face to face struck them with terror. Now on a cold winter's night, amid the chaotic Bethlehem census, the Son of God is born in a hidden stable where animals lodge for the night. God becomes man and shepherds and kings come to gaze into his eyes. Instead of power and authority they find vulnerability and trust. God trusted us enough to become one of us, to cast his lot with ours, to let us be responsible for protecting his Son in those tender first years of his life.

Each year Christmas Eve reminds us to keep looking again and again into the face of Jesus. When we are afraid, overwhelmed, troubled, suffering, in Jesus' face alone will we find the love and compassion that will soothe our anxious hearts. This face is the proof of God's love for us, for he became one of us. On Christmas Day we look into the crèche and gaze upon the Virgin and her child. But where will we find his face when we put away the Christmas decorations?

One day I was reading the Bible when I suddenly knew God was somehow gazing on me. As I allowed myself to be "seen," I was overwhelmed with a sense of the kindness and mercy of Jesus' eyes. I heard in my heart the words: "As long as we keep looking at each other, nothing else matters. I don't care about your faults and mistakes. Keep your eyes on me."

Oratio

Close your eyes. Picture yourself walking into the stable. A few animals huddle for warmth on the floor covered with straw. But in a corner, sheltered from the wind, a warm light glows. Go over and investigate. A young mother beckons you to come closer. She calls you by name. "I am glad you are here. I have been waiting for you. I knew you would come. Here is Jesus." Spend some time gazing into his eyes. Mary picks him up and asks you to help her by holding him. While you nestle Jesus in your arms, speak to him about your deepest needs. Then listen. Jesus will have something to say especially to you.

Contemplatio

Throughout the Christmas season, repeat the words Jesus says to you.

December 26 — Saint Stephen

⁛ ············ ⁛

Lectio

Matthew 10:17–22

Meditatio

> *"For it will not be you who speak*
> *but the Spirit of your Father speaking through you."*

We might suppose that the day after Christmas would bring us another cozy Gospel story of angels and shepherds or Magi traveling across countries, following the light of a star. But today, instead, we recall one of the first martyrs of the early Church—Saint Stephen.

Stephen's story seems to break rather abruptly into the Christmas season. The rage of the crowd and Stephen's violent martyrdom startle us. It seems so much at odds with the utter wonder and simplicity of God coming among us as a newborn baby. New hope was born among us, cause for great joy. The story of Stephen is given to us today as a challenge to bring this joy out into a world that often resists it.

As too soon the lights and decorations begin to come down around us and life quickly returns to more "ordinary" time, it can be difficult to live out the joy and hope that we celebrate each Christmas. When we experience moments of suffering or fear, the peacefulness of the crèche scene may seem very far away. But Jesus promises us that he will always be with us.

Just as Mary and Joseph lived each moment leading up to the birth of Jesus—and after—with trust in God's faithfulness, Jesus calls us to put our trust in him.

Oratio

Jesus, our world profoundly needs the peace and hope that we celebrate each year at Christmas. Send me your Spirit, that I might speak your words of peace in moments of pain and difficulty. Help me to trust in your promise to always be with me.

Contemplatio

"If God is for us, who can be against us?" (Rom 8:31)

December 27 — Saint John the Evangelist

❖ .... ❖

Lectio

John 20:1a, 2–8

Meditatio

> *"[H]e saw and believed."*

One cool, sunny morning, I was enjoying a good conversation over breakfast with a few sisters from my religious community. We were sitting near the window, and the sunlight streamed in at a particular slant, casting bright light on an otherwise imperceptible strand of a cobweb. Someone commented, "When the sunlight touches something, you can see what is otherwise hidden."

When light figuratively streams into our life as faith, what is hidden becomes manifest. Faith always reveals what the human eye cannot see but which the heart of a believer can perceive. We begin to "see" God, ourselves, others, and the world around us, whether in the ordinary or extraordinary circumstances of our life, in a new light.

Just three days ago, on Christmas Eve, we began celebrating Christ, the Light that has come to shine upon our darkness. Today's reading brings us to the resurrection, the fullness of Christ's light upon us. John, the beloved disciple, brings us from the darkness of the tomb to the light of faith.

As Peter and the beloved disciple peer into the tomb and see the burial cloths, the reality and light of the resurrection flood their being. John "saw and believed."

In the beginning of the First Letter of Saint John, we read: "what we have seen with our eyes, what we looked upon and touched with our hands concerns the Word of life—for the life was made visible ... what we have seen and heard we proclaim now to you" (1 Jn 1:1–3). Blessed are we, too, for we "see and hear" Christ in Scripture, in the Eucharist, in our neighbor, and in the community of believers. In the light of the gift of faith, we can "see" Christ everywhere. As the light of the sun allows us to see more clearly, so the light of faith can open up unimaginable dimensions of truth, beauty, and goodness around us!

Oratio

Thank you, God, for the gift of faith. In moments of darkness may faith be the invisible lantern to guide my steps. In moments of joy may faith allow me to share your light. Thank you for coming to dwell among us, to be our Light. Incarnate God, I adore you. I want to see you in all the circumstances of my life: cobwebs, world events, relationships, job, ministry, family, challenges, beauty ... everything! Increase my faith and increase my ability to see with new eyes. Lord, you are my one and true Light!

Contemplatio

May I see with the eyes of faith.

December 28 — Holy Innocents

⋮ ⋯⋯⋯⋯⋯ ⋮

Lectio

Matthew 2:13–18

Meditatio

> *"Joseph rose and took the child*
> *and his mother by night and departed for Egypt."*

Matthew's Gospel is the only Gospel that includes the account of the slaughter of the Holy Innocents and the flight of the Holy Family into Egypt. In choosing to include it, he foreshadows the cross from the start, reminding us that Jesus did not avoid our human suffering and pain—he was born right in the midst of it! Forced to flee into Egypt as refugees to escape the heinous and unjust actions of a historically cruel king, the Holy Family knew what it was to live in our imperfect and often dark world. They, too, suffered injustice and experienced the loneliness of being far from home.

In a world where headlines often tell of war, terror, persecution, and even genocide, we are painfully aware that our world is no more peaceful and utopian now than it was then. Political strife and injustice can be found on every side, and mothers continue to weep inconsolably for their children, born and unborn. This world torn with darkness and pain prods each one of us to question the areas of our own life where we may be contributing to violence—in any of its forms—through prejudice, lack of forgiveness, hatred, discrimination... No one of us is fully innocent. Each of us has places in our hearts that need the healing touch of the Christ Child.

And yet, ultimately, I believe Matthew relates these tragic events surrounding the birth of Christ to give us hope. Into the deep darkness of this night of sobbing and lamentation, when the cries of many mothers can be heard "weeping for … children" who are no more, the Christ has come. At the moment when we least expect it, our Deliverer, who will lead us to new freedom and hope, is born. Light has come into the world and the darkness cannot overcome it.

Oratio

Dear Lord, as I look back over the course of my own life, I am aware of my own areas of darkness and pain … perhaps even times when I felt abandoned or alone. I ask you to show me now how you were present in my moments of greatest suffering, bringing light into what may have seemed like total darkness. As I seek your presence there in the dark, I also ask you to reveal to me how I can bring that presence into our world today. Teach me how to radiate your peace and your love, so that I can become a source of your light for all who mourn.

Contemplatio

You are the Light of the World.

December 29

⁘ · · · · · · · · · · · ⁘

Lectio

Luke 2:22–35

Meditatio

> *"This man was righteous and devout, awaiting*
> *the consolation of Israel, and the holy Spirit was upon him."*

In this Gospel scene we contemplate Simeon, a godly man who anticipated the arrival of the Messiah. Simeon is praised highly in Sacred Scripture. An old man, he was filled with the Holy Spirit, and he longed for the coming of the Messiah. He is described as "righteous and devout"; clearly he was a man of prayer who knew the Hebrew Scriptures intimately. His frequent prayer made him sensitive to the inspirations of the Holy Spirit. Simeon's intimacy with God empowered him to recognize this child, carried in the arms of his mother, as the "glory for your people Israel."

Who knows how long Simeon waited to see the Messiah? As he grew older, he trusted that the Lord's promise was near at hand, and he anticipated meeting him with joy! Can we imagine the joy he felt as he held the child Jesus in his aged hands? After thousands of years of Israel's longing, his eyes were privileged to gaze upon the promised One. Simeon's mission was complete. God had satisfied his heart's desire.

In his canticle of prayer, Simeon holds the yearnings of both Jews and Gentiles. He first recognizes that this baby in his arms is God's gift to all people. Jesus will be a cause of contradiction, and he will suffer opposition and rejection. The Gospel tells us that Simeon speaks only to Mary, even though Joseph was present. Mary will share deeply in Jesus' suffering as his most faithful disciple.

How many wise Simeons (men and women) dwell in our families and churches! They are aged, perhaps, and younger as well. Their fidelity is a precious gift. Their wisdom helps us to recognize and appreciate God's revelation in our lives. Their encouragement supports us when we bear the cost of Christian discipleship. Who are the Simeons in your life? Ask them for the gift of their prayer and tap into their wisdom!

Oratio

Jesus, when Simeon gazed upon your face, his life reached its completion. All of Simeon's desires were fulfilled in you. Help me to recognize your coming in the persons whom I will meet this day—especially the poor and the troublesome. Open wide the thoughts and motives of my heart! Reveal how you are inviting me to grow as a Christian. May your Spirit support me when the cost of discipleship weighs me down. Mary, Mother of Jesus, pray for me and for all who struggle to be faithful to their Christian commitments.

Contemplatio

"My eyes have seen your salvation, which you prepared in sight of all the peoples...."

December 30

⁝· ············ ·⁝

Lectio

Luke 2:36–40

Meditatio

"And coming forward at that very time, she gave thanks to God...."

Today we are invited to join the Holy Family in a very intimate and sacred moment. We follow as they gently carry the Infant along the pathways and into the holy city of Jerusalem. Today the child, as the first-born Son, must be offered to God. This is a happy day for the parents of Jesus. They will perform the expected ritual with great joy and thanksgiving. God has entrusted them with such an unexpected treasure in this child.

As they approach the priest who will receive their Son, Mary and Joseph find themselves in a throng of other couples with their sons, other relatives who accompany them, and curious passersby. An old woman stands to the side, an obviously pious grandmother. Luke confirms their observation. She is Anna, daughter of Phanuel of Asher's tribe. Although the Gospel doesn't mention whether she had children or not, she has been widowed now for most of her life.

Anna has a special calling from God. She is a prophet. It is not recorded whether she ever prophesied before or after this day, but today she speaks for God, introducing the Christ Child to all who are present. And she continues throughout the ages to proclaim him to all who are awaiting redemption, whenever this passage of Luke is read. Not only does she proclaim him to us with her words, but her life was a prophecy of the life he was beginning that day. Jesus, we are told, went on to grow and become strong, filled with wisdom and the favor of God. Anna had spent her years foreshadowing this. "She never left the temple, but worshiped night and day with fasting and prayer." She invites us today not to stay in the temple, but to have hearts attuned to God, hearts that, by their very attentiveness, worship night and day. Then, not just in this season, but every day, our lives will be a prophecy of the Lord's coming.

Oratio

Lord, let me live each day before you that I may be aware of your approach. You come most often in weakness, in poverty, in ordinariness, from the midst of my everyday routine. Prepare me to witness to you as Anna was prepared, by a life of prayerfulness lived in your presence. May my life be filled with your wisdom, strength, and favor today and always. Amen.

Contemplatio

"... and [she] spoke about the child to all who were awaiting the redemption of Jerusalem."

December 31

⁘ ⋯⋯⋯⋯ ⁙

Lectio

John 1:1–18

Meditatio

> *"No one has ever seen God. The only Son, God,*
> *who is at the Father's side, has revealed him."*

Have you ever had the chance to see a famous person whom you really wanted to meet? Perhaps a sports star, an actor, a civil leader, or someone else you almost idolized? What was it like for you? How did you feel when you saw your hero in person?

I still recall vividly how thrilled I was to see the Pope in person for the first time, when John Paul II celebrated Mass at Yankee Stadium in 1979. After the Mass, he rode around the stadium in the Popemobile, smiling and waving, and I got to see him up close. I felt ecstatic, swept up in the moment and the cheering crowd. It buoyed my spirit for quite a while.

Such things, though, can't even begin to compare with what it is like to see God. That's what John is telling us in the prologue to his Gospel. God gave us the greatest gift possible when he sent his Son to earth to suffer and die for us.

Perhaps because it is so familiar to us, we can easily take for granted the incredible gift of the Incarnation. We can hardly begin to grasp the reality of this mystery. But ponder it for a moment. Even though we cannot fully understand it, we can thank God the Father for sending us his Son. He came to this earth to become one of us, to save us from our sins, and to lead us to eternal life with him.

One simple way to acknowledge the mystery it so pray the Angelus.* This simple prayer reminds us of what the Incarnation means. "… the Word became flesh and made his dwelling among us…." Hail Mary….

Oratio

Lord Jesus, I thank you for the amazing gift you gave us by becoming flesh and dwelling among us. Help me to understand this mystery, even if only a little. Pour out your Holy Spirit on me so that I might grasp with my heart what I cannot grasp with my mind. I thank you for being the light of life. Enlighten us all with your truth. You came to earth as our Way, our Truth, and our Life. I believe in you and I love you. Amen.

Contemplatio

"From his fullness we have all received, grace in place of grace…."

---

* For a beautiful video presentation of the Angelus, check out: http://calltoprayer.blogspot.com

Holy Family
Sunday in the Octave of Christmas — A

:⋅ ⋯⋯⋯ ⋅:

Lectio

Matthew 2:13–15, 19–23

Meditatio

> *"The angel of the Lord appeared to Joseph in a dream."*

In this Gospel excerpt, Matthew presents Jesus as a Moses figure. Moses was the great leader and savior of the Jews. He led them out of slavery in Egypt and formed them into a people. But as an infant, Moses' life was endangered when Pharaoh wanted to kill all the Hebrew baby boys. Jesus faces the same danger from Herod. So God directs Joseph to flee into Egypt. When it is safe to come back, Matthew again alludes to the parallel with Moses in the quote, "Out of Egypt I called my son."

Joseph plays an important role in all this. He doesn't speak, but we see him go into action. Twice in this short passage, Matthew reports what the angel told Joseph: "Rise, take the child and his mother...." In each case, Joseph responds in the same way: "Joseph rose and took the child and his mother...." He acted promptly and did what God wanted him to do. He didn't complain or object. We don't know much about Joseph, who is often overlooked. But we do know that he carried out God's will. He protected Jesus and Mary and provided for their needs. Because of this role, he is often invoked as the patron saint of those who seek jobs or need other economic help.

We might think that Joseph had it easy. After all, an angel appeared to him to tell him what to do. But it wasn't as if God spelled out all the details. The Gospel says, "Joseph was afraid to go back there." He had to figure out for himself where he could safely bring his family to live. That took initiative. God directs us in similar ways. If we listen at prayer, the Holy Spirit will inspire us about concrete decisions in our lives. Then, like Joseph, we can act according to God's will.

Oratio

For your prayer, talk to Saint Joseph about the needs in your life right now.

Contemplatio

Saint Joseph, pray for us!

Holy Family
Sunday in the Octave of Christmas — B

⁖ ············ ⁙

Lectio

Luke 2:22–40

Meditatio

> *"They took him … to present him to the Lord.…"*

Every time I have pictured this scene in my head, I see Mary as she stands cradling a newborn Jesus (he is just over a month old judging from when the rite of purification was to be held according to the Torah). Saint Joseph stands behind Mary—he's always in the background. I also picture Simeon holding his arms out to receive the child so as to perform the rite, and Anna pointing at Jesus while talking to strangers. In my mind it has always been Mary who presents Jesus, while Joseph stands in the background. But if we look at the whole scene, that is not the case. It is all of them— Mary, Joseph, Simeon, and Anna—who together are presenting Jesus both to the Lord and to the world. In other words, it is an act of a whole community.

Today, more than two thousand years after Jesus' birth, God continues to use the entire community of believers to help the Light reach all nations. In a quick snapshot of the scene mentioned above, we see Mary and Joseph presenting Jesus just as parents today are called to present Jesus to their children, welcoming him and the Gospel message into their homes. We see Simeon, representative of those who have dedicated their lives to following God either through religious life or priesthood. Lastly, we see Anna, a woman who can represent all of us who through our baptism are called to evangelize—she "spoke about the child to all." Here, the entire Christian community is called to proclaim the greatest gift this world has ever received. No one person can do it alone, just as Mary alone could not present her child to the Lord. It is the community working together that enables Jesus to truly live among us.

Oratio

Lord, I thank you for the call to be an active member of your body, the Church. Also, with deep gratitude, I pray for all those who have given and continue to give of themselves so that I may know you. Today I wish to put at your disposal the gifts and talents you have given me. Help me this day and every day to live my vocation generously, so that others may come to know you through my words and actions, and that I may come to know you better through theirs.

Contemplatio

Thank you, gracious Lord, for the call to communion and community.

Holy Family
Sunday in the Octave of Christmas — C

∴ ·········· ∴

Lectio

Luke 2:41–52

Meditatio

"Why were you looking for me?"

Tension and misunderstanding even in the Holy Family! If that doesn't give us courage, what will? Our human limitations make us susceptible to anxiety, confusion, and misunderstandings. But if we keep our spiritual compass pointed at God, we will try to make allowances for our individual differences and move ahead, as Jesus and Mary did after this incident.

Why did Jesus remain in Jerusalem? I like to think he was responding to an impulse of the Holy Spirit, who comes and goes freely (see Jn 3:8). Perhaps this was the first strong movement of the Spirit within Jesus. He may have been as surprised by the impulse as Mary and Joseph were by his actions!

Have you ever done something without understanding why? Did you learn afterward that your choice was the best one? There's so much we don't understand about God's activity in the lives of his free creatures. Human life is a mystery in which God has chosen to be involved, even though we must continue to reflect, discern, and use our free will. God is with us; God is for us.

Let's savor the mystery, alert for the Spirit's activity in our midst. Mary did that—pondering over and over the extraordinary happenings that took place in her ordinary life. She loved, trusted, sought to understand. And whenever understanding did not come, she must have fallen back on faith.

When we reflect on this, Mary becomes very easy to relate to. She faced many of the difficulties that we may face, such as the challenge of trying to make ends meet and the nagging anxiety for the safety of loved ones. In the face of gross injustice, Mary must have struggled to understand God's ways as we often struggle. Although Mary is our Mother, she is also our sister in faith.

Oratio

Mary, Mother of Jesus and my Mother—Mary, my sister in faith—help me to recognize the Spirit speaking to me through words, circumstances, events, my state of health, my emotions… Help me to discern his message. Obtain for me the grace to respond with faith, dedication, and love as you did. Pray for me, that I may be an ever more faithful disciple of Jesus, your Son and my Brother.

Contemplatio

"… his mother kept all these things in her heart."

January 1
Solemnity of Mary, Mother of God

:• ············ •:

Lectio

Luke 2:16–21

Meditatio

> *"... the message that had been told them...."*

It may seem strange at first to focus on a fragment of a sentence. Since this fragment is repeated three times, I think it may hold the central message for us, the one we are meant to remember. Luke is a good teacher—repetition, they say, is the most effective way to teach.

The shepherds "went in haste" to Bethlehem after they saw and heard the angels announcing the birth of the Savior. After Mary learned that the Savior would be born of her, she, too, "traveled in haste" to visit her cousin Elizabeth. It seems that in both cases the "message that had been told them" caused the hearers to quickly respond to it.

When the shepherds arrive and see "Mary and Joseph, and the infant lying in the manger," they retell "the message that had been told them." Those who hear the message "were amazed by what had been told them...." Then the shepherds return home, "glorifying and praising God" because what they witnessed was "just as it had been told to them."

Like the shepherds, we have heard the message. But unlike the shepherds, we have not been able to verify it in the same way. So the Gospel stresses that "what had been told them" was indeed true, and in this we find our verification.

This message is so powerful that it drives Mary and the shepherds to respond immediately and with haste. They have no time to lose—they have to do something with that message. Similarly, if we allow the message to "move" us, we will be able to see and hear that the "message that we have been told" is indeed true. Where will we know it? We will know it in our hearts, just as Mary did.

Oratio

Dear Lord, sometimes I have to admit that I am bored and unmoved by the message I have heard. I seem so far removed from the stories that meant so much to the people involved in them. Help me to hear the message with a new heart so that I too will be moved by it. Help me to understand what it means that a Savior has been born for me.

Contemplatio

"Blessed be the Lord, the God of Israel, for he has visited and brought redemption to his people" (Lk 1:68).

January 2 — before Epiphany

$\vdots \cdots \cdots \cdots \cdot\vdots$

Lectio

John 1:19–28

Meditatio

> *"There is one among you whom you do not recognize . . ."*

"I am not the Christ!" John the Baptist bellows. It is not so much a denial as it is a proclamation: "He is here! He is near! He is in your very midst." Meanwhile, in the crowd of nameless sinners, a Galilean carpenter waits his turn for the symbolic washing, probably too far from shore to hear the exchange. "There is one among you whom you do not recognize—the one who is coming after me." John, too, had to admit: "I did not know him, but the one who sent me to baptize with water told me, 'On whomever you see the Spirit come down and remain, he is the one.'"

Three years later, at supper with his followers, Jesus will ask reproachfully: "Have I been with you for so long a time and you still do not know me?" Even after the resurrection, Mary Magdalen saw him "but did not know it was Jesus."

When I start to obsess over an experience or situation, examining it in minute detail, tracking cause and effect . . . could it be that "there is one whom I do not recognize"? Could it be that in every circumstance, the Word is *dwelling among us*, even if unrecognized?

To "recognize" him means more than acknowledging intellectually *who* Jesus is. That is only a first step along the way, an invitation to *receive* him in the concrete situations of my life, and so enter into his relationship with the Father, thus becoming a child of God as the Prologue of John's Gospel promised. To really recognize Jesus means continually discovering that we are unable to box him in according to our own categories (categories that, conveniently, keep us in charge of the experience!); to recognize him is to surrender to a reality that, as John will later say, surpasses us because it pre-existed us.

He *has* come, but if we do not recognize him, it is still Advent.

Oratio

Lord, sometimes I don't recognize you in painful circumstances because I don't want to associate you with what is hurtful (despite seeing the image of your cross); or I don't recognize you in my successes because I'm too busy celebrating to reflect on the way my talents and skills are your gifts.

In these waning days of the Christmas season, I want to begin to recognize you in the graced experiences of my daily life. I want to renew my faith that you never leave us on our own. Despite circumstances that might distract me, I will acknowledge and recognize you as the one in whom I live and who makes everything beautiful in its time (see Eccl 3:11).

Contemplatio

The Word was made flesh and dwelt among us.

January 3 — if before Epiphany

∴ · · · · · · · · · · · · ∴

Lectio

John 1:29–34

Meditatio

"Behold the Lamb of God who takes away the sins of the world."

When we hear these familiar words, we probably think immediately of how we pray them during the Eucharistic Celebration. The priest holds up the bread and wine that have become the Body and Blood of Christ and repeats these words once spoken by John the Baptist. Also, immediately before that, the title "Lamb of God" is used as we sing or pray the litany during the breaking of the bread: "Lamb of God, you take away the sins of the world, have mercy on us."

Since we are in the Christmas season, the phrase "Lamb of God" might make us think about the lambs and sheep belonging to the shepherds of Bethlehem. But at John the Baptist's time, how did the people around him understand his words? What did he mean by calling Jesus the "Lamb of God"? The people listening to John would most likely have thought of the lambs that were offered in sacrifice. They would think of the paschal lamb, which was slaughtered at Passover. They knew that lambs offered in sacrifice had to be "without blemish."

John's listeners might have remembered Isaiah's prophesy about the servant of the Lord who was led "like a lamb to the slaughter." "Because he surrendered himself to death, and was counted among the wicked, he shall take away the sins of many and win pardon for their offenses" (Is 53:7, 12).

So the words of John the Baptist, coming as they do in a reading of the Christmas season, hint at the future suffering and death of Jesus, his pure sacrifice that will take away our sins. Many of Jesus' followers had a hard time with the idea of a suffering Messiah, even when Jesus predicted his passion point blank. But John was given this understanding. He saw in some way that the Messiah will be a suffering servant of the Lord, in fulfillment of the Scriptures.

Oratio

Jesus, so often I pray using the phrase "Lamb of God" without thinking about what it means. I want to make it a prayer of gratitude for your self-giving love. Your sacrifice, your death, has brought me life and salvation. Help me remember this each time I hear the words, "Behold the Lamb of God, who takes away the sins of the world."

Contemplatio

Behold the Lamb of God!

January 4 — if before Epiphany

⁝ · · · · · · · · · · · · ⁝

Lectio

John 1:35–42

Meditatio

"Behold the Lamb of God"

In my prayer life lately God has invited me to pause and ponder more profoundly the concepts of hearing and listening. So much goes on around us: we are bombarded by noise, voices, and words. But do we really listen to the messages we hear? How do they affect us?

The sights and sounds of the Christmas season still surround our hearts and homes in this New Year. But our secular and consumerist society all too quickly puts this holy season aside. Yet we stay near the crib with Mary and Joseph and ponder the wonder and meaning of the infant Christ Child.

This Gospel reading gives us a moment to pause and listen. Liturgically we are journeying toward Epiphany, which means manifestation. When Jesus appears on the scene, John the Baptist recognizes and acknowledges him, "Behold the Lamb of God."

The Jewish people were awaiting the Messiah, so on hearing these words two of John's disciples followed Jesus.

Turning to them he asked, "What are you looking for?" They replied, "Where are you staying?" He invited them, "Come and see."

The two disciples were captivated by the words of Jesus. They heard his invitation to come, listened to his message, and became Jesus' first followers. Andrew excitedly sought out his brother Peter, exclaiming they had found the Messiah, and he brought him to the Lord. The Gospel message isn't meant to be kept secret but to be shared.

We listen to God's voice as he speaks to us in the present moment and invites us to act on what we hear. We are called to share his love and goodness with others by the witness of our lives.

Oratio

Lord, you speak to me through your word and give me grace through the sacraments. Infuse your spirit of wisdom and understanding within me. As I listen to your voice within my heart, you beckon me to *come*, *hear*, and *listen* to your invitation. Today may I witness to you in my words, actions, and encounters with family members, co-workers, and acquaintances.

Contemplatio

"It is no longer I who live, but Christ who lives in me" (Gal 2:20).

January 5 — if before Epiphany

⠶ ⸱⸱⸱⸱⸱⸱⸱⸱⸱⸱⸱ ⸱⸱

Lectio

John 1:43–51

Meditatio

> *"Rabbi, you are the Son of God. . . ."*

The Prologue of John's Gospel offers us this jewel: "To those who did accept him he gave power to become children of God" (Jn 1:12). In these days we are reading the first chapter of John, which presents us with one person after another, all with their own stories. They were given the invitation to accept Jesus and to become God's children. These same accounts of the calling of the apostles will be read in the liturgy later in the year. At that time, we will most probably fix our gaze on the apostles. We will look at them, as it were, through the eyes of Jesus. We might even feel with Jesus, perhaps, a bit of trepidation as he waits to see if they will accept his invitation.

In these days of the Christmas season, instead, we find ourselves contemplatively gazing at *Jesus* through the eyes of the apostles. As these men hear the invitation of Jesus, they respond simply—not many words, no plans, no weighing of the pros and cons of following this Rabbi. They don't consider what it will cost them. They simply and quietly contemplate this gentle teacher who was addressing them. Philip brings Nathanael to see Jesus. Right away Nathanael discovers how he is already known by the Master before him, who holds him with the gentle acceptance of his gaze. Nathanael responded with adoration—not excitement, anxiety, or sorrow, but adoration. Christmas is an extended practice of adoration, wonder, waiting, listening, silence. . . . During these days we ourselves learn to gaze anew on Jesus, we find ourselves drawn to follow him without plans, fears, self-protection. We learn only the response of yes.

Oratio

Jesus . . . Savior . . . Lord . . . Teacher . . . King . . . God. You have become one with us that we might become one again with God. I hear you asking me if I will follow you. Yes. My answer is yes. Now and forever. Always yes.

Contemplatio

"To those who did accept him he gave power to become children of God" (Jn 1:12).

January 6 — if before Epiphany

⁘ ⋯⋯⋯⋯ ⁘

Lectio

Mark 1:7–11

Meditatio

> *"One mightier than I is coming after me. . . ."*

John the Baptist always seemed to have a sense of urgency. So when he cried out in the desert, "One mightier than I is coming after me," people streamed out to the desert to receive John's baptism of repentance. As they listened to him, new hope stirred in their hearts.

John reminded them of the prophets of old, who urged the people to turn away from their infidelity and back to the Living God. With his leather belt and clothes made of camel's hair, he seemed like the prophet Elijah (see 2 Kings 1:8). Could John be the long-desired Messiah?

John was clear about his own role and strictly adhered to it. He stated bluntly, "I am not the Christ" (Jn 1:20). He could have drawn the crowd to himself for his own vain purposes, but he did not. Instead, he helped them to recognize Jesus as the One who was coming. I see in John an evangelizer's role model. He proclaimed the message with passion and pointed others to Christ. John didn't seek anything for himself but compared himself to the best man at a wedding who rejoices for the bridegroom (see Jn 3:29).

When Jesus joined the throngs of people at the Jordan, I imagine the mysterious looks he exchanged with John. The Baptist protested that he was not worthy to baptize Jesus. But Jesus made it clear that he wanted to receive this outward sign of repentance and forgiveness. One day he would create a new people of God through the life-giving baptism with the Holy Spirit, but first he would bear the burden of sin and God's judgment on their behalf.

When he came up out of the water, Jesus saw the heavens break open, and the Spirit descended on him. A mighty voice announced: "You are my beloved Son; with you I am well pleased."

Oratio

Jesus, I behold this marvelous revelation of your baptism. Anointed in the Spirit, you now begin the saving mission entrusted to you by the Father. The first covenant was given in the desert of Sinai. So too, here in the Judean wilderness you set about restoring our relationship as beloved sons and daughters of your Heavenly Father.

Renew me in your Spirit and consecrate me for mission. May your love and truth shine through me so that others may discover in you the Truth that saves. Make me a radiant and compelling witness, willing to walk with you all the way to Calvary.

Contemplatio

"You are my beloved Son; with you I am well pleased."

January 7 — if before Epiphany

Lectio

John 2:1–11

Meditatio

"Do whatever he tells you."

At the wedding feast in Cana, the married couple fade into the background while Jesus takes over. He's only a guest, yet he steps in to give orders to the servants and miraculously provides wine for the feast. And he does this after telling his mother it's not his concern. He even rebuffs her request with a puzzling remark about his "hour." If you knew nothing about Jesus, all of this would probably make you wonder, "Just who does he think he is?"

That's precisely the point. Who is Jesus? Who does he think he is? Who do *I* think he is? The Gospel writer wants us to "wonder" about Jesus and ultimately come to faith. He tells us that Jesus "revealed his glory, and his disciples began to believe in him" (Jn 2:11). Everything Jesus does is meant to reveal the mystery of who he is.

As Christians, we know through faith who Jesus is: he is the Son of God, our Savior. But being so familiar with Jesus, we might miss the astonishing significance of what this really means. Perhaps the marriage theme can give us a new way of looking at him. The abundance of wine gives us an important clue, because the prophets often used wine to signify the coming messianic times: "On that day the mountains will drip new wine . . ." (Joel 4:18). At Cana, Jesus appears symbolically as the bridegroom of the messianic wedding feast. The wine of Cana can symbolize the gifts Christ gives us in the new covenant. We can rejoice because by becoming flesh, God has in a sense "married" the human race.

For that gift we owe thanks to Mary. When Jesus begins his mission, his relationship to Mary changes. She is still present to him in some way, but she must feel the pain of letting him go—the pain every good parent feels when a child leaves home. But Mary, as always, does whatever God asks. Her words to the servants, "Do whatever he tells you," are the last words she speaks in the Gospel, a fitting last will and testament. They evoke what the people of Israel said when sealing the covenant, "We will do everything that the LORD has told us" (Ex 24:3). In this light, Mary appears as the one who perfectly embodies Israel's response to the covenant. Mary, a woman of Israel and daughter of Zion, shows us how to do God's will in our lives.

Oratio

Mary, my Mother, intercede for me and present my requests to Jesus, your beloved Son. I ask for the strength to always do what Jesus asks.

Contemplatio

". . . and the mother of Jesus was there."

Epiphany — A, B, C

∴ · · · · · · · · · · · ∵

Lectio

Matthew 2:1–12

Meditatio

> *"Then they opened their treasures and offered him gifts*
> *of gold, frankincense, and myrrh."*

Christmas is the time of gift-giving, and in the Eastern Churches Epiphany is the day for exchanging gifts in remembrance of the visit of the magi. Traditionally we have known these men as kings, wisemen, and, as they are called in today's reading, magi. Scholars debate who they were, how many they were, and where they came from. Tradition has decided they were three, hailing from different countries, definitely learned men since they studied the stars; definitely as wealthy as kings, due to the gifts they brought. The early Church historian, Bede the Venerable, gave them names: Melchior, Gaspar, and Balthasar.

Whether or not all these details are historically correct, we can certainly learn from the example of these mysterious visitors. They knew about the significance of the announced Messiah; they read the Scriptures; they sought insight. They followed the evident sign and acted upon inspiration. When they found the child, "they prostrated themselves and did him homage" first, and "then they opened their treasures and offered him gifts." Is this the order we follow at Christmas? It is our adoration that Jesus desires even before we present our gifts. And what do we offer to him from our treasures? The magi gave gold, frankincense, and myrrh. We offer all that is precious to us, what makes us who we are. This is our gold. We offer all that is sweet, our joys and pleasures, which have the fragrance of frankincense. We offer our sufferings and disappointments, as bitter as myrrh.

What became of the gifts that the magi gave the Christ child? No one knows. However, we know that our gold, frankincense, and myrrh will be accepted and blessed by our Lord, and then returned to our keeping to be brought back into our lives. And we continue to offer them daily with grateful hearts.

Oratio

Dear Lord, born daily in my heart, I come before you in adoration because you are my blessed hope. You are the star that guides me; you are the direction, the way I must go. You send innumerable signs and place helpful persons along my path. You await my faltering prayers as well as my awestruck silence. I place before you everything I am and have. I will not hold back or hide your gifts to me, but I will humbly lay them before you. May I feel your hand in blessing as I offer you my all.

Contemplatio

"They were overjoyed at seeing the star."

Monday after Epiphany — or January 7

∴ · · · · · · · · · · · · ∴

Lectio

Matthew 4:12–17, 23–25

Meditatio

> *"From that time on, Jesus began to preach. . . ."*

Today we see Jesus beginning his public ministry. After hearing of John's arrest, Jesus withdrew to Galilee. But he moved from Nazareth to Capernaum with purpose, not out of fear. Matthew highlights the prophecy of Isaiah: the people of Galilee would see a great light. Jesus brought that light, which would shine in that place overshadowed by death. His words are simple and direct: "Repent, for the Kingdom of heaven is at hand."

Touring all of Galilee, Jesus proclaims the Good News with courage and conviction. He calls the people to repentance so that they will be able to receive the news about the Kingdom of heaven. Repentance brings about a purity of heart that makes people open to grace. Bringing his mission of mercy to all, Jesus also cures the sick and frees the possessed. News of this spreads rapidly, and great crowds begin to follow him.

The Son of God was made manifest to the world—that is, to us—and we must take this Good News on the road.

This is what the time after Epiphany asks of each Christian. Don't just speak the message, but get into the business of curing the sick and freeing those bound. How we do this depends on our circumstances, on how much sickness exists, on how many around us are in the grip of evil. How do I bring the Good News to people today? How can I lighten the shadows? I can't do it on my own power, but only with the help of grace. Jesus will be at my side to give me strength.

Oratio

Lord Jesus, fill me with your courage and commitment, your grace. May your words be my words, so that when I speak my words may become your instrument to lead others to you. Teach me to be available to those who live in the shadows of doubt and even in despair. Transform me so that all you have given me may manifest you. May crowds be drawn to you by how I live my discipleship. Amen.

Contemplatio

"And great crowds . . . followed him."

Tuesday after Epiphany — or January 8

∴ ⋯⋯⋯⋯ ∴

Lectio

Mark 6:34–44

Meditatio

> *"Are we to buy two hundred days' wages worth of food*
> *and give it to them to eat?"*

Stingy thinking. Even after having been in the presence of Love for a time now, the apostles were worried about having to open their purse for this crowd of hungry people. Maybe they were wondering, *Will we have enough for ourselves? Where will we go to get enough food? Imagine the work involved in bringing the food back to the crowd!* And he apostles were probably hungry themselves. It seemed easier to them to send the people away to fend for themselves.

The apostle John in the first reading tells us: "God sent his only-begotten Son into the world so that we might have life through him." What a marvel of generosity! The Father didn't just provide us a meal. He gave us his dearest Son. He turned over to us, he put into our hands, the Word that most completely expresses his love. God trusted us with his heart! God wasn't stingy. God wanted us to have life, to live forever, to once more be united to him, the source of life and love. To use an image from Saint Augustine, God sent to us a purse full of the coins of his mercy. It was a little purse, the tiny baby found in the crib, Son of Mary and yet Son of God. The Father opened the purse and freely poured these coins into the world to supply for all our needs: to heal us, guide us, love us, teach us, forgive us, transform us, and comfort us.

In these days before Ordinary Time begins, the Church gives us a final opportunity to marvel at the gift of the babe in the manger. In this gift, we see how God's love for us in Christ has shaped our own life and all of history. Each of the sacraments we receive is a concrete way in which God's life grows in us more profoundly. God spends the coins of mercy on us, and we can then turn and liberally spend them in kindness and compassion for others. No, we must not be stingy in our thinking or worry about ourselves. The invitation of Christmas is to open our hearts to give away what we have received in Christ: mercy, love, and compassion.

Oratio

Father, department stores have already packed away their decorations and moved on to a new selling season. Christmas trees have been set out on street curbs and Christmas lights no longer twinkle as brightly. Don't let Christmas die in my heart . . . your Christmas . . . the Christmas I am meant to live all year long through actions of mercy and love and compassion.

Contemplatio

Shape my life, generous God, with your mercy, love, and compassion.

Wednesday after Epiphany — or January 9

∴ · · · · · · · · · · · · ∴

Lectio

Mark 6:45–52

Meditatio

"Take courage, it is I, do not be afraid!"

We are now in the middle of the last week of the Christmas season. The liturgy continues to shift our focus from the baby in Bethlehem to the grown Jesus performing miracles in Galilee. In today's Gospel, Jesus walks on the water toward the disciples, who are "tossed about while rowing." The disciples are terrified! But Jesus does not let them remain terrified. He immediately reassures them with three little, yet powerful, words: "It is I."

In these words we can see the heart of Jesus' message during his entire earthly life. He came to earth to tell us: *It is I. I am Emmanuel. I am God-with-you. I am present in every part of your life, and with me, you do not need to be afraid of anything.* These words are the thread that begins with Jesus' birth, the ultimate miracle of God-with-us. This thread runs through his life and every miracle, culminating in his death and resurrection.

Stormy seas and unwieldy boats may seem to be the farthest thing from Christmas that we could imagine. But in fact this moment on the sea is a Christmas moment, because it reinforces and convinces us of the Christmas message. All of Jesus' miracles are Christmas moments, because each of them repeats, "It is I." Some miracles whisper this message and others shout it, but they all clearly proclaim it.

The disciples and nature alike respond to Jesus' words. The wind abates, and the disciples are "completely astounded." We, too, can spend today in wondering gratitude for all the ways that Jesus tells us, "It is I."

Oratio

Jesus, sometimes storms rage in the seas of my life; sometimes calm settles. I need you to walk across these seas toward me and get into my boat. I need to hear you say, "It is I, do not be afraid!" Thank you for the countless ways you remain present to me every day. Thank you for the ways you surprise me. Whether today is stormy or calm, I want to welcome the gift of your presence and be present to you as well. Amen.

Contemplatio

"It is I—I am with you."

Thursday after Epiphany — or January 10

∴ · · · · · · · · · · · · ∴

Lectio

Luke 4:14–22

Meditatio

"They looked intently at him."

Even without today's technology, news traveled fast in first-century Galilee. Reports about Jesus quickly spread throughout the region. Imagine the anticipation and excitement as Jesus strode into the synagogue that morning.

Returning to Nazareth, where he had been brought up, meant seeing many relatives and friends at the synagogue. Much to their delight, the young man stood up, unrolled the scroll, and began to read: "The Spirit of the Lord is upon me. . . ."

Something marvelous was happening. The words seemed so natural coming from Jesus' own lips: "he has anointed me to bring glad tidings to the poor . . . to proclaim liberty to captives . . . recovery of sight to the blind." Although the people had so often heard these words of Isaiah, today they leapt from the scroll and deeply stirred their hearts. As Jesus finished reading and sat down, *"the eyes of all in the synagogue looked intently at him."*

What were they thinking as they looked at him? *Who is this that speaks with such authority? How can this be? We know this man . . . he is one of us.* Did their very familiarity with Jesus somehow stifle their willingness to truly *see* him?

Perhaps my invitation today is similarly to pause and *look intently* at Jesus. What is he saying to me? What does he want to reveal to me? I recall the words Jesus later spoke: "Blessed are the eyes that *see* what you see" (Lk 10:23). I am moved to desire to see with inner eyes the depths of Jesus' love for me. I desire a deeper relationship with Jesus and his Father. I want to remain in that look of love Jesus so willingly returns.

Oratio

Thank you, Lord, for the many ways you continue to reveal yourself to me. Help me to see with the inner eyes of faith and to lovingly accept your invitation to welcome the gift of your divine Presence, both in word and sacrament.

Help me to listen more deeply to your inspirations. May these illumine and guide my decisions and actions as I pattern my life on yours. Grant that I might enjoy the full vision of your glory one day in heaven, together with the angels and saints and all my loved ones!

Contemplatio

"Blessed are the eyes that *see* what you see."

Friday after Epiphany — or January 11

∴ ⋯⋯⋯ ∴

Lectio

Luke 5:12–16

Meditatio

> *"Jesus stretched out his hand, touched him, and said,*
> *'I do will it. Be made clean.'"*

Other lepers probably lived in the same town as the one who was healed in today's Gospel reading. Did they also go out to see Jesus and be healed? We don't know. Perhaps some did, but it is likely that some simply dismissed the wild tales they had been hearing. *Who was this itinerant preacher anyway?* they may have thought. *Why should I bother going after him?*

It amazes us that they missed such a great opportunity. Who wouldn't want to be healed? But doesn't the same thing still happen today? Jesus lives among us; he is present in many ways. One of the most significant ways he is present is at the Eucharistic celebration. His presence in the Eucharist remains after Mass. If we so desire, we can visit him there and pray before the tabernacle. Just as he healed the leper, Jesus still heals today, in different ways.

The healing may not be a physical one. But he bestows gifts of grace very freely. All we need is faith in him. Those who believe deeply will benefit greatly. By faith we can touch

Christ spiritually, just as he touched the leper physically. The same power that made Jesus heal is still available to us today. This is a deep mystery, one that we need to ponder.

We are now in the week between the Epiphany and the Baptism of the Lord. Both of those mysteries manifest Jesus; they show us who he is. Yet his mystery can only be grasped by faith. This faith is not just something abstract, but a living faith that will lead us to change our lives. But what if I don't want to change? That can be my obstacle. Change is often painful. After the leper was healed, he rejoiced. But then he had to change his whole way of life. He wasn't a leper anymore. Perhaps it was hard to reintegrate himself into the life of the village. But surely it was worth it, just as it is worth it to come before Jesus and receive his healing touch today.

Oratio

Lord Jesus, I thank you for the many gifts of grace you have given me so freely. I want to receive these and follow you with deeper faith. I thank you in particular for the healing grace you give us through the Holy Eucharist. When I come into your eucharistic presence, help me to listen to the words you whisper into my heart. Take away my fears and lead me into the fullness of life with you.

Contemplatio

"Lord, if you wish, you can make me clean."

Saturday after Epiphany — or January 12

∴ .... ∴

Lectio

John 3:22–30

Meditatio

> *". . . this joy of mine has been made complete."*

I find it fascinating that in the Gospels of Luke and John the same emotion—joy—is used to describe John the Baptist's reaction to Jesus. This joy must have made quite an impression on those who witnessed the events surrounding John.

The Gospel of Luke describes John's reaction to Jesus when they were both in the womb. "And how does this happen to me," his mother Elizabeth said, "that the mother of my Lord should come to me? For at the moment the sound of your greeting reached my ears, the infant in my womb leaped for joy" (Lk 1:43–44).

In the Gospel of John, the Baptist himself describes how he feels about Jesus. He is filled with joy when he hears remote news about the Lord. That joy runs so deeply in him that he must have surprised those following him. The text seems to hint that John's disciples expect him to be jealous of Jesus. "Remember the man you testified about? Well, everyone's going to *him* now. . . ."

Perhaps *we* can be jealous of *John*. So often we maintain an image of God that inspires fear rather than joy. But for John, Jesus is the Bridegroom at the happiest moment of his life. Who can't be joyful in the presence of a man about to wed the one he loves? Each of us who awaits the coming of the Lord can have the same joy that John did. If we do, then we too will likely react very differently to the circumstances we find ourselves in. The only thing that will matter for us is that Jesus is waiting in the wings, and that, like John, we have been chosen to testify to him.

Oratio

Jesus, thank you for reminding me that you are the Bridegroom of humanity. I am blessed to be numbered among those who can testify to you. I want to be more like John, who allowed himself to be solely motivated by this reality. As I wait for you to fully reveal yourself to me, may I too rejoice at the slightest sound I hear that reminds me of you!

Contemplatio

May I be filled with joy at the sound of your voice!

Baptism of the Lord — A

∴ .... ∴

Lectio

Matthew 3:13–17

Meditatio

> *"I need to be baptized by you, and yet you are coming to me?"*

With the feast of the Baptism of the Lord we liturgically move into the long season of Ordinary Time. These thirty four weeks are interrupted only by the seasons of Lent and Easter. On a more mundane level, we leave behind the blessed season of contemplation of the Incarnation of the Son of God who set up his tent among us. We now move into daily living out the consequences of this event. This Gospel passage describing the baptism of Jesus by John is a perfect hinge between the two seasons. Jesus and John must have known each other to some extent, since these two cousins were only a few months apart in age. At the very least they knew *about* each other. They must have known at some level what each was doing, what values moved them. Jesus' appearance at the Jordan River disconcerted John. John saw the One for whom he had been sent to prepare the way now standing before him, asking to be baptized. They were each fulfilling God's plan. Jesus came to be baptized so that our sins would be buried in Jordan's waters. He who was sinless presented himself to be cleansed in John's baptism of conversion. He who was the fire of God's approach to us was hidden in the meek request for purification.

The Feast of the Baptism of the Lord gently pulls us away from the manger and sends us out into our lives of discipleship to live our own baptism: a program of honest self-appraisal, confident trust in God's mercy shown to us in Jesus, commitment to conversion, and a renewed awareness that God calls us "beloved." As the Father commissioned Jesus to go forth into his public mission, so you and I are now sent to be "of Christ" in our families, in our workplace, in schools, on soccer fields, and in grocery stores, board rooms, and courtrooms, nursing homes, and hospitals. In short, everywhere we go can be transformed by the presence of Christ when we live out our baptism.

Oratio

Jesus, beloved of the Father, you and John the Baptist played out your lives on the stage of the Father's love for humanity effected through the history of our salvation. As I begin Ordinary Time, I too am an actor in this drama of the Father's mercy. I commit myself now, as you committed yourself in your baptism at the river Jordan, to complete surrender to the Father's plan so that he may use me for the salvation of the world. Amen.

Contemplatio

Father, I commit myself now to complete surrender to your plan.

Baptism of the Lord — B

∴ ⋯⋯⋯⋯ ∴

Lectio

Mark 1:7–11

Meditatio

> *"One mightier than I is coming. . . ."*

The Feast of the Baptism of the Lord is the last day of the Christmas season, yet it takes the place of the First Sunday of Ordinary Time. This reading from the Gospel according to Mark definitely launches us into Ordinary Time and beyond.

The child in the manger whom we have been contemplating for weeks is the one John describes as "mightier than I." That description brings us into the public ministry of Jesus as a fully grown itinerant teacher, worker of miracles, and master to his followers. Then, two sentences later, we have jumped forward not only through the public ministry, but also beyond the passion, death, and resurrection to Pentecost, as John foretells: "He will baptize you with the Holy Spirit."

The baptism of Jesus represents a threshold in his life, between his hidden life (the years of his carpentry work in Nazareth) and his public ministry. A threshold marks an end and a beginning. It is meant to be a stepping stone to what lies beyond. It's a place to reach, perhaps to pause, and then to cross. It's not a place to stay, to make one's home, or even to camp out.

Can you imagine what the world would be like if Jesus had decided to enjoy the quiet life of carpentry and stay out of the spotlight? What if he hadn't wanted a public ministry full of controversy, opposition, and the hardships of an itinerant life? Where would we be if he had refused to pass over this threshold and the even more difficult ones that followed? Fortunately, we don't have to worry about that. Jesus did come, was baptized by John, and the Father was well pleased.

Oratio

Jesus, give me the strength and courage I need to follow the Father's plan for my life and to move from what is comfortable and familiar to the new things that are asked of me. Sometimes it is hard enough to cross the threshold into a new day—moving from sleep to getting out of bed in the morning. But since I am going where you lead—where you have already gone before me—I have nothing to fear and nothing to lose. I trust you will guide me my whole life and, at its end, bring me over the threshold of death into new life.

Contemplatio

Lead me, Lord.

Baptism of the Lord — C

:• · · · · · · · · · · · •:

Lectio

Luke 3:15–16, 21–22

Meditatio

> *"The people were filled with expectation,*
> *and all were asking in their hearts whether John might be the Christ."*

So many things happen in this passage: John meets Jesus and baptizes him, the voice of God the Father speaks from heaven, and the Spirit appears as a dove. But the first line in particular draws me in: "The people were filled with expectation. . . ." Imagine how much hope they must have felt. They had been waiting for the Messiah and are thinking: *John may be the one we've been waiting for. Finally, the Messiah has come!* But John tells them: "one mightier than I is coming."

Imagine their questions: *If John is not the Messiah, then who is the Messiah and when will he come?* Their hopes have been dashed. So now where do they go? Sometimes we, too, can have high expectations for something close to our hearts. But when things turn out differently than we had hoped, we may be at a complete loss. It's as if we need to hit the reset button in order to get our bearings. I would prefer to know what's coming next instead of being surprised. But our God is a God of surprises, which are always better than any plan I could have dreamed up on my own.

Although "the people were filled with expectation," they were confused when John said he was not the Messiah. But imagine how amazed they were to hear the Father's words after Jesus was baptized: "You are my beloved Son; with you I am well pleased." That was like their reset button. Their hearts were again filled not only with expectation, but also with hope and joy in Jesus, the Messiah. As we too rejoice in Jesus' baptism, we can also be grateful for our own baptism and listen to the words the Father speaks to each of us.

Oratio

Jesus, thank you for the great gift of the sacrament of Baptism. May everyone feel the Father's joy for them as he says, "This is my beloved son/daughter, with you I am well pleased." May we live out of the promise given to us in our baptism; may we remember that, as your children, you love us and call us to relationship with you.

Contemplatio

I am a beloved child of God.

List of Contributors

:• ············ •:

BOOKS & MEDIA

The Daughters of St. Paul operate book and media centers at the following addresses. Visit, call, or write the one nearest you today, or find us at www.pauline.org.

CALIFORNIA

3908 Sepulveda Blvd, Culver City, CA 90230	310-397-8676
935 Brewster Avenue, Redwood City, CA 94063	650-369-4230
5945 Balboa Avenue, San Diego, CA 92111	858-565-9181

FLORIDA

145 S.W. 107th Avenue, Miami, FL 33174	305-559-6715

HAWAII

1143 Bishop Street, Honolulu, HI 96813	808-521-2731

ILLINOIS

172 North Michigan Avenue, Chicago, IL 60601	312-346-4228

LOUISIANA

4403 Veterans Memorial Blvd, Metairie, LA 70006	504-887-7631

MASSACHUSETTS

885 Providence Hwy, Dedham, MA 02026	781-326-5385

MISSOURI

9804 Watson Road, St. Louis, MO 63126	314-965-3512

NEW YORK

64 W. 38th Street, New York, NY 10018	212-754-1110

SOUTH CAROLINA

243 King Street, Charleston, SC 29401	843-577-0175

TEXAS

Currently no book center; for parish exhibits or outreach evangelization, contact: 210-569-0500, or SanAntonio@paulinemedia.com, or P.O. Box 761416, San Antonio, TX 78245

VIRGINIA

1025 King Street, Alexandria, VA 22314	703-549-3806

CANADA

3022 Dufferin Street, Toronto, ON M6B 3T5	416-781-9131

¡También somos su fuente para libros,
videos y música en español!